Simple Phonetic
English Spelling

Simple Phonetic English Spelling

Introduction to **Simpel-Fonetik**,
the Single-Sound-per-Letter Writing Method

by Allan Kiisk

A **practical** and **proven** solution
to the spelling and pronunciation problems
of the English language

Tate Publishing & Enterprises

Published by Tate Publishing & Enterprises, LLC
127 E. Trade Center Terrace | Mustang, Oklahoma 73064 USA
1.888.361.9473 | www.tatepublishing.com

Tate Publishing is committed to excellence in the publishing industry. The company reflects the philosophy established by the founders, based on Psalm 68:11,
"The Lord gave the word and great was the company of those who published it."

Book design copyright © 2008 by Tate Publishing, LLC. All rights reserved.
Cover design by Leah LeFlore
Interior design by Nathan Harmony

Published in the United States of America

ISBN: 978-1-60462-899-9
1. Language Arts & Discipline: Alphabet
2. Phonetics & Phonics/Spelling
08.04.09

Contents

Introduction

Purpose of the Book

English words, in most instances, are very difficult to convert from spoken sounds to writing. Everyone has problems with English spelling. The main reason is that more than half of the letters in the English alphabet have multiple sounds. And some letters are used for no sounds at all. English spelling is very complicated.

Most people, especially those who have grown up and lived with the English language, have accepted the spelling problem as a fait accompli. They have become accustomed to the habit of looking up words in the dictionary, just as I, the author, had to look up the spelling for *fait accompli*. The problem is made worse by the fact that one needs to know how the word is spelled, at least approximately, to look it up in the dictionary.

English is becoming a global language. Millions of people all over the world are learning English. They learn it by reading every word, trying to pronounce each word based on what they read. They don't have the benefit of having heard that word spoken before, as is the case with students whose mother tongue is English. They have to look up each pronunciation in the dictionary after they read the word, or have someone tell them how to pronounce each word.

They have learned that one can not trust the letters used in writing a word to indicate how to pronounce that word.

And when they know how to pronounce a word, often they don't know how to write it, because there are many ways to write a word.

They all ask: "Why can't you write a word the way it sounds? Why can't you read a word the way it is written?"

The writing of this book was motivated by empathy for everyone who is trying to learn the English language, the desire to give answers to the above questions, and to do away with the problems associated with the present spelling of English words.

Another motivation was to support the acceptance of the English language as a global language. The biggest obstacle to acceptance is that the English spelling is so difficult, so nonsensical. It makes people ridicule, dislike, even detest the English language. This book shows how to get rid of that obstacle.

This book presents the most reasonable, practical, and proven method of converting English spoken words into writing, and converting the writing back to spoken words.

The method is based on the principle of having only one sound, a single sound, for each letter. It is a principle used very successfully in other European languages.

The proposed phonetic spelling method is based on the use of the existing English alphabet with the addition of two more letters, letters that are used in other languages.

The sounds derived for the revised alphabet happen to be in agreement with the international alphabet used by airline pilots and other communicators worldwide.

This book shows the derivation of the proposed phonetic spelling method and establishes the rules for its use. It is an introduction to what the author has named the *Simpel-Fonetik* method of writing and reading English words.

The Author's Background

You might ask: "What background do you, the author of this book, have that makes you qualified and credible as a critic and a promoter of improvements to the English language?" I'll try to answer that.

I am fluent in three languages.

My mother tongue is Estonian, a language in the Finno-Ugric group of languages, very similar to Finnish. I graduated from an Estonian high school (secondary school) while living in Germany as a World War II refugee.

If you are not familiar with Eastern Europe, let me point out that Estonia is a small country just south of Finland. It is slightly bigger than Switzerland or Netherlands, but it has a smaller population, approximately 1.4 million people.

The second language that I became fluent in was German. I learned German because I lived in Germany for nine years, including two years of service in the U.S. Army in Germany.

The third language, English, is now my everyday-use language. My university education was in English. All my professional activities have been in English.

I have studied other languages, but not enough to gain fluency.

I studied Latin for four years and can still recite the first chapter of Caesar's "De Bello Gallico" ("Gallic Wars") from memory. I have not used Latin for conversation, but the knowledge of Latin has helped me with other languages, because many words are based on Latin roots.

I know a little bit of Russian and can pronounce Russian words almost without an accent. That is because when I was very young, my parents switched from speaking Estonian to Russian whenever they did not want us children to understand what they were saying. But it did not take us long to understand some Russian. Later, I learned how to read Russian, at least enough to read road signs so that I could drive my car in Russia.

Whenever I visited Finland, I spoke Estonian because the two languages are very similar. For simple conversations, I didn't need to use English.

I have taken lessons in Spanish, but not enough to be fluent. But living in California, I am constantly exposed to Spanish.

I am most comfortable speaking English. I consider myself an excellent speller, but that did not happen by accident. I have spent an exorbitant amount of time looking up words in the dictionary. And I still do.

I did not grow up with the English language. I did not pick it up from my parents. I had to learn it in school, from various teachers and textbooks. While I was learning English, I was communicating in two other languages: German, and the phonetically written Estonian. That situation, I feel, gave me special advantages, skills, and experience for analyzing the English spelling problems and coming up with solutions.

And I feel that my professional background as an electrical engineer, researcher, and university professor helps to assure that the conclusions developed here are based on thorough, competent analysis.

Problems in Writing English

Problems in Writing English

I like the English language. I can't explain why. I like it in spite of the fact that it has many problems.

There is a lack of logic and consistency throughout the English language. One problem, for example, is that forming plurals is illogical and inconsistent. Why is the plural of *foot feet*, but the plural of *boot* is not *beet*? The plural of *man* is *men* but the plural of *pan* is not *pen*. The plural of *box* is *boxes*, but the plural of *ox* is *oxen*.

Another example is that forming past tenses is illogical. Why is it *ring, rang, rung,* and *bring, brought, brought,* and *wring, wrung, wrung*? All those words have the same base word *ring* in them.

There are many problems in the English language that need to be corrected, but I will ignore the ones I just mentioned. In this book, I will concentrate only on one problem—the worst problem.

The worst problem is the writing, reading, and pronouncing of English words. The spelling is inconsistent, illogical, and incoherent. There is no basic system; no sensible, simple rules. Here are a few examples:

In the English language, the letter *a* is used to represent many different sounds. In pronouncing the words *far, ant, all, ago, make, head, read, foam, fear, pair,* and *earn,* you'll hear that in each word the letter *a* has a different sound.

The *a* sound, as in *far,* is also represented by other letters. For example, the letter *u* in the words *up* and *fun,* and the letter *o* in *rob* and *some.*

The words *cough, rough, though, through,* and *plough* are pronounced quite differently, even though they all have the same *ough* base.

And very similar words, such as *heard* and *beard, rose* and *lose, card* and *ward, word* and *sword,* are pronounced differently.

There are same-sounding words written in two or more different ways. For example, when you say the word *write,* it can also be heard and written as *right* and *rite.* You can say *meat,* but it will sound exactly the same as *meet* and *mete.* You can say *ate* but it can also mean *eight.* Here are a few more examples:

Cite – site – sight   *I – eye – aye*   *I'll – isle – aisle*   *nose – knows*
one – won   *two – too – to*   *were – wear – where*   *you – ewe*

In the present spelling, when dealing with similar-sounding words, letters are changed or added to distinguish their meanings when they are written down without expecting the pronunciation to change. This practice has been a major contributor to the spelling and pronunciation problems of the English language.

And there are words that you just don't know how to pronounce until you get more information. Take the word *read.* It can be pronounced either as *reed* or *red* if it is in the present or past tense.

Another example is the word *wind.* It is pronounced one way when it refers to weather, another way when it refers to a clock.

The word *lead* is pronounced *leed* if it means to guide, *led* if it refers to the black stuff inside the pencil.

In the English language, we have so-called "silent letters." We write *knee,* but we don't pronounce the *k*. We write *know* but pronounce it as *no*; the letters *k* and *w* are silent. We write *weight,* but the letters *gh* are silent. We write *damn*, but the *n* is silent.

And sometimes the letter *e* is placed at the end of the word such as *rout,* to become *route*, to signify a different meaning of the word, but the letter *e* is silent; it is not pronounced.

It makes no sense to have silent letters. To add silent letters, for whatever reason, is a very bad idea. Someone just learning the language will not know which letter is silent and which should be pronounced.

Years ago, there was an attempt to improve the spelling of the word *through.* In that word, the four letters *ough* are used to represent the sound *u*. Some people started using the spelling *thru* in place of *through*. But the change was not officially sanctioned. *Thru* is listed in the dictionary as the informal version of *through*. It should have been listed as the preferred version.

Most of us who have spent the time to learn all the peculiarities of the English spelling have learned to tolerate the problems. Some Americans and British people, and others whose mother tongue is English, may wonder why so many people get worked up over the terrible writing aspect of English. "Why don't they just accept the "unique" or "romantic" or "historic" nature of English?" they might ask. I'll explain why.

We live in an age of computers and high technology. The fields of science, engineering, and mathematics have great importance in our daily lives. Those fields require logical and organized thinking. Those fields have provided technological advances because developments are based on the buildup of knowledge in a logical and organized way. For example, each mathematical symbol has only one meaning. Each chemical symbol represents one clearly defined item. Each letter in the Ohm's Law, $V = I \times R$, is associated with a clearly defined meaning. In Morse code, each letter has one, and only one, code of dots and dashes assigned to it. In computer programming, each code, each combination of ones and zeros, has an unambiguous meaning or action associated with it.

Therefore, an educated person would expect that there would be one letter, or at least the same combination of letters, for each sound. That would be logical. That would make sense. That would make the language much easier to learn. That would also make the language more compatible with science and engineering.

As an example, speech recognition—the automatic electronic conversion of voiced sounds, or speech, to writing—is much easier to implement when there is only one sound for each letter. Presently, with the English language, speech recognition is done on the basis of words, using a limited number of specially selected words.

This illogical spelling situation is frustrating not only to scientifically oriented people, but also to those who are familiar with other languages that are more logically organized.

I remember seeing how frustrated my mother, a schoolteacher, was when she was trying to learn English. She was fluent in Estonian, Russian, and German. She was already used to learning languages. But she never got used to English spelling.

There were many words that she was frustrated with, but the one that really got to her was the word *colonel*. She pronounced that word the way she saw it, as consisting of the basic word *colon* with the *el* as in *elk* added to it. She could not grasp the fact that the word *colonel* was supposed to be pronounced the same way as *kernel*, as in *kernel of corn*. Her favorite saying was that in English they write *cat* and pronounce *dog*.

In phonetic writing, such as what is used in the Estonian, Finnish, and other languages, every sound has only one letter associated with it, and every letter has only one sound. You see a letter and you know how to sound it out.

In the writing of those languages it is unheard of to have a silent letter (pun intended).

When you see a group of letters, as in a word, you sound out each letter in that group, and … you've just said the word. You pronounced the word that those letters formed. If you can read and pronounce individual letters, you can read words and know exactly how to pronounce each word.

In the dictionaries of the languages that use phonetic writing there is no pronunciation guidance. It is not needed. That space in the dictionary is used for other information. The dictionary writers don't have to deal with pronunciation guidance. The schools don't have to teach pronunciation; they don't need to spend time on that subject.

An additional great advantage of phonetic writing is that if you know how to pronounce a word correctly, you know how to write it. You enunciate each sound in the word and then write a letter for each sound that you heard in your enunciation.

In Estonia, for example, there are no spelling textbooks. Estonians don't need to study spelling. The question "How do you spell that?" is used only for foreign words.

In English-speaking countries, much time is spent on learning how to spell correctly. All through one's life one must look up words in the dictionary to see how they are spelled or pronounced. To an Estonian, that seems like a great waste of time.

An Estonian beginning to learn English knows that English is the most important language in the world. He knows that the world's best universities use the English language. Most of the world's technical advancements have come from places where English is the main language. He expects that English is at least as well organized and logical as the Estonian language.

And then he runs into words like *through*. And he learns that the letter *a* can be pronounced in eleven or more different ways. And that all the other vowels have no single sounds assigned to them, and that even the consonants have inconsistent pronunciations, and that some letters are not pronounced at all. He finds that he needs to spend a lot of time trying to look up pronunciations and spellings in the dictionary. And he discovers that in addition to the English alphabet, he has to learn the International Phonetic Alphabet to decipher the pronunciation of English words.

This person can't help but think: *Why? With all the advancements in the English-speaking world, why is the English writing so backward, so illogical, so disorganized, so difficult to learn? Can't it be improved? Couldn't someone come up with an improvement to make it at least as easy to write as Estonian?*

Why can't the principles of writing used in other languages, the phonetically written languages, be applied to English?

The answer is that a phonetic writing system similar to what is used in other phonetically written languages *can* be applied to the English language. It is entirely possible for English to become a language that can be easily converted from speaking to writing and from writing to speaking without having to memorize how to spell every word.

I understand that a person who is familiar with the history of the English language and with all the efforts that have been made in the past to improve the English spelling will be skeptical about what I just claimed. Many smart and famous people, including Andrew Carnegie, President Theodore Roosevelt, Melvil Dewey, and George Bernhard Shaw, tried to improve the English spelling. They did not succeed.

I am well aware of that. I have looked into their proposals and the proposals by many others. Some proposals that I have seen were ridiculous. Others were sound, but did not go far enough, or were inconsistent or illogical in some way.

What am I proposing to make English words easy to spell and pronounce? In what way is my proposed writing method better than those proposed before?

I'll explain.

Proposed Solution

Proposed Solution

In the world of music there are many different instruments playing many different sounds. In a symphony concert they all know exactly what to play, what sounds to produce, because they follow sheet music where each sound is represented by a symbol, a separate and distinct symbol, a note.

Sounds of music are often combined into chords. Chords could be viewed as being equivalent to words. Words are combined from individual letters and spoken sounds; chords are combined from individual musical notes and instrument or vocal sounds.

The whole world is familiar with musical notation. It is simple and logical. If you show me a note on sheet music, I can go to the piano and produce that sound. There is no confusion, no uncertainty, no need to check some musical sound dictionary to see if that sound goes with that notation. Musicians from the U.S. and the U.K. can go to other countries and play in their orchestras. Musicians from other countries come to play and conduct orchestras in the U.S. and the U.K. It is all possible because musical notation is so well standardized on one sound per note and one note per sound.

Couldn't we do the same thing with spoken sounds?

It would be wonderful if all of us, at least in the countries that use the Latin alphabet, could standardize the spoken sounds the same way as the musical notes. Then, just imagine, in addition to being able to play the songs, we could sing the songs that are on the sheet music, songs from different countries in different languages. We might not understand the words, but we all could sing together, singers from different countries. We would not have to translate the English words into a phonetic version that others would know how to pronounce, and the English speakers would know how to pronounce the words of songs of other languages.

This visualization seems a bit unrealistic, maybe too much to hope for, but we could visualize it as a goal. We can start moving toward the goal by taking certain steps.

A great step would be to have a standard method of writing spoken sounds, similar to musical sounds—one sound per symbol. Many languages—I mentioned the Estonian language as an example—have already standardized the sounds for each letter. The letters used in the Estonian language are in agreement with the International Alphabet, also known as the NATO Alphabet.

Please note that the International Alphabet is different from the International Phonetic Alphabet, also referred to as the IPA. I will use the term *NATO Alphabet* when there is a possibility of confusion between the two. The NATO, or International, Alphabet will be discussed further in the chapter titled "International Alphabet."

The English language also needs to take the step of standardizing the sounds for each letter. The English speakers *do* use the NATO alphabet for sounding out letters in international communications, but the English spelling is not in conformance with it. The English spelling needs to join the process of standardization. That would cause a huge advancement in international relations.

Once the English language standardizes its letter sounds, more languages will follow. Languages that are presently partially phonetic will become fully phonetic.

I visualize that some day an American can read Estonian, Finnish, German, and other languages and pronounce their words, and people from those countries can read and pronounce English words, without taking language lessons. There would be no more agonizing over the spelling and pronunciation of the multitude of words and expressions that have originated in English-speaking countries. More and more English words will be adopted by other countries, and the English speakers can readily adopt words from other countries that use the same phonetic spelling. That process will lead to better communication and understanding among people, more togetherness, and a movement toward global unity.

That, in my opinion, is entirely feasible. It can happen, and it should happen.

But these lofty thoughts must not let us lose track of the main reason for standardizing the spelling to a single sound per letter: To simplify the spelling and pronunciation of English.

The big benefit will be that when you see a written word, you can sound it out letter by letter, which will result in pronouncing the word. You do not need to look up the pronunciation of a word in a dictionary. The spelling of the word will be its own pronunciation guide or key.

A phonetic alphabet provides a second great benefit: It simplifies the spelling of words. If one knows a word and knows how to pronounce it, he can slowly enunciate that word, listen to the individual sounds making up that word, assign a letter to each sound, and thus write the word down.

How should we come up with such an alphabet? Should we

scrap what we have now and start from scratch? Or should we try to work with what we have?

The International Phonetic Alphabet (IPA) has been suggested by some people for use with the English language. It is a truly phonetic alphabet, used for the purpose of identifying the sounds used in all languages. To accomplish that, the IPA uses many—too many—strange letters and symbols. It was not designed to replace the Latin alphabet. I don't think we need such an elaborate alphabet. It would not be practical. It would be too big a change, too much to learn, and too different from other languages.

Let's look at phonetic alphabets and writing systems in existence that are based on the Latin alphabet. I look at them as simplified phonetic alphabets, to distinguish from the truly phonetic IPA alphabet. Those alphabets do not try to represent every spoken sound to every minor detail, as does the IPA. They cover the basic sounds in the language, and they accept the fact that some people will pronounce words differently anyway, no matter how accurately a sound is represented by a symbol.

The phonetic alphabets that I am referring to are the alphabets of the Estonian and Finnish languages—the best examples of phonetic writing—and the alphabets of other languages that may not be as phonetic but are similar to them. I will use those alphabets as an experience base for improving the writing of the English language.

The goal is to come up with a phonetic alphabet that is easy to use and has the minimum number of letters.

Now, let's look through the English alphabet, letter by letter, and see what can stay as used presently and what needs to be changed or added. Once we have a phonetic alphabet, we can establish a simple phonetic writing system that is suitable for the English language.

As is done in other phonetic languages, we shall follow the rule:

Each letter shall represent only one spoken sound.

Revising the Alphabet

The Good Letters

I have concluded that out of the twenty-six letters in the present English alphabet, ten letters do not need any change. They are just fine the way they are used now. Each of them is being used to represent only one spoken sound. Those letters are:

B D F K L M N P V Z

Let's look more closely at each of those letters. I'll list the letter and some sample words associated with that letter.

B – big, rib, bravo
D – dog, wind, madam
F – fit, soft, alfa
K – king, pink, Karin
L – leg, kilt, hello
M – mint, minimum, samba
N – no, sin, Anna
P – pet, top, opponent
V – vivid, rivet, TV
Z – zest, zebra, zip

Multi-Sound Letters

Every one of the remaining sixteen letters of the English twenty-six-letter alphabet has more than one spoken sound associated with it. Those letters are:

A C E G H I J O Q R S T U W X Y

I'll list each letter and give samples of words where the different sounds of that same letter occur. I suggest you read those words aloud.

A – far, ant, all, ago, make, head, read, foam, fear, pair, earn

C – can, cent, chip

E – enter, me, new, sew, learn, route (e is silent)

G – go, gin

H – hotel, photo, chin, right

I – in, mine, sir, lieu, timbre

J – join, junta

O – on, one, two, hot, women, colonel, broad

Q – quick, liquor

R – ring, far

S – sit, sugar

T – tip, nature

U – put, but, unit, turn, laugh, bought

W – win, write, low

X – sex, xylophone

Y – yes, my, typical, Olympia

Making Choices

Now we need to select the proper single sound for each of the multi-sound letters.

The letter *a* has many different sounds in the present English. Which one of those sounds should be assigned to it? What criteria should be used in the selection?

The main, most important criterion should be standardization. If a letter is known to have a certain sound in other languages, especially in other phonetic languages, we should choose that same sound. That will make English easier to learn and use, especially by those who are already familiar with the Latin alphabet. And it will make it easier for English speakers to learn other languages. It will help maintain English as an international language.

Another consideration should be: How great an impact does the change have on the present speakers and writers of English? Is there a compromise that would reduce the impact but would still adhere to the rule of one sound per letter?

One could come up with other criteria, such as considering the percentage of use in present English. For example, in the case of the letter *a*, the pronunciation as in *fat* or *man* may appear to be more popular. Should that outweigh the fact that the letter *a*, as in *art* or *architect*, is pretty much the standard sound for *a* in other languages?

Next, I'll look at each multiple-sound letter and choose one of the sounds as the only sound for that letter.

I'll do it in two stages. First, I'll list the letters with easy choices. They require very little explanation or justification. Then I'll list and analyze the letters where the choice is more difficult or controversial.

Easy Choices

The words following each letter illustrate how that letter should be pronounced and what sound was chosen for that letter.

E – as in *enter, echo, mend*

The choice is based on the international standard usage. The other often used sound as in *me* will be handled by the letter *i*. The letter *u* will be used in *new*, an *o* in *sew*, and a new letter will be established for the *ea* sound in *learn*.

G – as in *go, get, log*

The choice is in agreement with the IPA and all the languages that I am familiar with. And I would not dare to propose that the writing of *God* or *golf* be changed.

When *g* is used in words like *gin* and *register*, where it sounds like *j* in *Jim*, the letter *j*, or whatever is chosen to represent that *j* sound, should be used in place of *g*.

H – as in *hotel, hello, hit*

The use of *h*, as in *photo* and *laugh*, will be handled by the letter *f*.

It is interesting to note that as of August 2006, the German language did away with the use of *ph* wherever the letter *f* will do the job. The English language should do the same.

The use of *h* in combination with the letter *c*, in words like *chin* and *rich*, will be discussed further when the letter C comes up for discussion.

I – as in *India, win, kilt*

Even experienced English speakers are not sure if the *I* in *Iraq* and *Iran* should be pronounced as in *India* or as in *Ireland*. This choice will settle it. The IPA and much of the rest of the world pronounce *i* as in *India*.

The use of *i* in words like *mine* will be modified. The letters *ai* will be used in place of *i*. The word *lieu* will use the vowel *u* and *sir* will require a new letter.

The word *timber*—it refers to wood—has good phonetic spelling. But there is a similar word *timbre*, a musical term, where the only spelling difference is that the last two letters are reversed. In that word the letter *i* is pronounced as the *a* in *ant*. We'll have to substitute the appropriate letter. You will read more about it in the discussion of the letter *A*.

O – as in *on, off, logo*

Where the letter *o* is used for a sound similar to *u*, as in *two*, the letter *u* will be used in its place.

In words like *fowl* and *foul*—another case of two spellings of the same spoken word—where the *o* sound does not even exist, the other appropriate vowel or vowels, such as *au,* will be substituted.

Q – Not needed, except for classical English and foreign words

In English, the letter *q* is nearly always used together with the letter *u.* The combination of *q* and *u* is pronounced as if there was the letter *w* involved. And, of course, one can clearly hear the sound of the letter *k.*

As an example, pronounce the word *wit.* Now pronounce the same word with the letter *k* in front—*kwit.* It sounds exactly like *quit.*

You can do the same experiment with *west.* Add the letter *k* in front of *west,* making it *kwest.* Pronounce it. It sounds exactly like *quest.*

Therefore, the words *quit* and *quest* could and should be written as *kwit* and *kwest.* And the word *quick* should be written as *kwik* and *quota* as *kwota.*

In words such as *liquor* and *parquet* there is no *w* sound. The *qu* should be replaced by just *k.*

R – as in *ring, Romeo, rest*

The use of *r* as a silent letter in words like *far, fire, part,* and *tear* must be avoided. Wherever the letter *r* appears—or any letter—it should be sounded out.

The use of the letter *r* is discussed further in another chapter.

S – as in *sit, kiss, past*

There is a problem in the use of the letter *s* in words such as *sugar* or *sure.* In those words the letter *h* is needed to bring the spelling to agreement with the spoken sounds as is properly done in words like *shore, shop, cash, and finish*. So *sugar* and *sure* should be spelled *shugar* and *shur*. The silent *e* is deleted.

In borrowed foreign words such as *faux pas* and *apropos*, the letter *s* is silent; it is not sounded out. And there are other letters that are not sounded out. Both expressions come from French. The word *faux* is pronounced as *fo*, and *pas* as *pa*. My College Dictionary defines *faux pas* as "an embarrassing blunder." That is a very *apropos* definition. One could use *faux pas* as an example of an embarrassing blunder in spelling, a so-called "horrible example," to show how not to convert spoken sounds into letters.

Just think about it: If the French would have a stronger influence on the English language, the words *go* and *no* would be spelled *gaux* and *naux*.

T – as in *tip, ten, tentative*

The letter *t* should not be used in words like *creation* and *mention*. In those words the sound of *t* is not present. One can only hear the sounds of *s* and *h*.

In words such as *nature* and *feature* the sound of *t* is present. So a *t* belongs there. But there are also *s* and *h* sounds. More about that in another chapter.

U – as in *put, full, true*

The chosen sound agrees with the *u* sound in many other languages.

The letter *u* used in words like *but, cup, hut*, and *pulp* has a sound similar to *a* in *art* and *tar*. Therefore, *u* should not be used in those words.

The letter *u* should not be used as in *laugh* and *bought*, because the chosen sound of *u*, as in *put*, is not heard in those words.

There is a slight problem with words like *unit, butte,* and *mural*. The letter *u* belongs there, but there is something missing. Look at the words *yule* and *Yuma*. They show that the letter *y* (or the IPA designated letter *j*) belongs also in front of the *u* in *unit, butte,* and *mural*. We'll address that later.

W – as in *win, west, swim*

The letter *w* is pronounced in German and some other languages as the English *v*. Estonians don't have *w* at all; they get along fine with just the letter *v*. The sound that the English speakers have given to the letter *w* is unique. It does not exist in other languages, as far as I know. There doesn't exist a good combination of English alphabet letters to represent the *w*, so one must leave the letter *w* as it is, pronounced as in *win*.

W often appears in the English spelling as a silent letter. Examples are words *write, wrist,* and *wrinkle*. Let's drop the *w* from those words. They will still be pronounced the same way.

In the word *low* there is no *w* sound. But there is a *u* sound. A *u* should be in place of the *w*.

In the word *law* there is no *w* sound. The *aw* is pronounced as the two *o*'s in *door*. So why not write *loo*? (The use of long-sounding vowels is discussed in the chapter titled "Double Letters.")

X – Not needed, except for classical English and foreign words

The letter *x* represents the sounds produced by sounding out the letters *k* and *s* close together.

The use of the letter *x* causes problems in phonetic spelling. It causes inconsistencies in spelling. Often there is a letter *s* added to a word to make it a plural form or another verb form. Look at the words *sink, mink,* and *link.* Adding the *s* for plural form gives *sinks, minks,* and *links.* Those words sound like they should be spelled *sinx, minx,* and *linx,* following the example of *jinx, lynx,* and *sphinx.*

To establish consistency, we should use one or the other, either the *x* or the *ks.* But for words where the plural is formed by adding an *s* to a *k,* as in *mink,* it does not make sense to convert the *ks* to an *x* just for the plural form.

A much better solution is to stick with the one-sound-per-letter rule and use *ks* wherever that sound occurs and wherever the letter *x* appears.

The word *sex* could be written as *seks* and no one would have any problems with it—I mean, pronouncing it.

In a few words, such as *xylophone* and *xenophobia,* the *x* should be substituted by either *z* or *s.*

Difficult Choices

The choices are more difficult for the letters A, C, J, and Y. In the following, for each of those letters I will indicate what sound was chosen and then discuss the reasons.

A, a

Pronounce as in *art* and *car*

I have chosen the single sound for the letter *a* to be the sound as in *art* and *car*. It is the worldwide standard sound for that letter. The Estonians, Finns, Germans, French, Italians, Spanish, Portuguese, Russians—even the Hawaiians and the Vietnamese—they all use the *art* and *car* sound for *a*. And so does the IPA (International Phonetic Alphabet).

Someone might argue that in the English language, especially as spoken by the Americans, there are more words where *a* is pronounced as in *ant* than are words where *a* sounds as in *art*. Americans even pronounce the word *aunt* as *ant;* the British don't. So why shouldn't the *a* as in *ant* pronunciation be chosen as the single use?

The answer is that the actual sound of *a* as in *art* occurs more frequently than the sound of *a* as in *ant*. That is because many other letters are used to convey the *a* as in *art* sound.

As a small sampling, let's look at the words *cup, under, up, foundry, fowl, my, five, dry, money, light, kite, funny, shut, rob*…I could go on and on. In all those words one hears the *a* as in *art* sound, yet the letter *a* does not even appear in any of those words.

The fact that the letter *a* is not used where it should be makes the English spelling so difficult. But what makes it even worse, much worse, is that when it is used, it can represent any one of at least eleven different sounds.

We just discussed the basic *a* as in *art* sound. Here are some other sounds conveyed by the letter *a*:

(1) In the words *ant, can, lamp, rat*, and many other words, the letter *a* is pronounced as the IPA letter that looks like the letters *a* and *e* back-to-back (Æ, æ). The dictionaries that use the IPA phonetics use that letter to represent the *a* as in *ant* sound.

In the Estonian, Finnish, Swedish, and other languages, the letter *ä* (an *a* with two dots on it) is used for that sound. The German language uses the letter *ä*, but it does not sound quite like the English *a* as in *ant*.

There is no question that a new letter is needed. The only question is which letter should be chosen. The choice is between the IPA's *æ* or the *ä*. I'll mention that the symbol @, presently used as *at* in e-mail addresses, has been suggested for the *a* as in *ant* sound, but I think that was done without the knowledge that the letter *ä* is already in popular use.

I am proposing to use the letter *ä* as the substitute for the letter *a* in words like *ant, can, lamp*, and *rat*. It is a well-established letter and the easiest to write. Ä, *ä* would become an additional letter in the English alphabet.

This choice is discussed further in the chapter titled "New Letters."

(2) In the words *all, salt, fault, malt,* and many similar words, the letter *a* is pronounced as *o* in *for, door,* or *floor.* I propose that we use the letter *o,* or double *o (oo)* in all cases where *a* is used for the *o* sound.

(3) In the words *make, play,* and many similar words, the letter *a* is pronounced as the combination of *e* and *i* sounds, as in the words *veil* and *freight.* I propose that we substitute *ei* for *a* in those words. *Make* and *play* will become *meik* and *plei.*

(4) In words such as *head* and *bread,* the letter *a* adds nothing to the pronunciation. The words would sound the same if we just wrote *hed* and *bred.* I propose that we delete the *a* in those words.

(5) In words like *foam* and *road,* the letter *a* has the *u* sound. So why not use the letter *u* in place of *a.* We could write *foum* and *roud.*

(6) In many words, such as *ago, another, awhile,* and *alike,* the *a* has a sound that is not represented by another letter in the present English alphabet.

A longer version of the similar sound occurs in *word, occurs, turn, stir, fir, learn,* and *her.*

In other languages, including Estonian, Finnish, Swedish, German, and others, that sound as in *her* is represented by the letter *ö (o* with two dots).

I recommend that we introduce the letter *Ö, ö* into the English alphabet.

The letter *ö* is discussed further in the chapter titled "New Letters."

C, c

This letter is not needed, except for classical English or foreign words

The letter *c* is presently used for three sounds: (1) the sound of *k* as in *can, scone,* and *school,* (2) the sound of *s* as in *cent, citrus,* and *civilian,* and (3) in combination with the letter *h,* as *ch,* to represent the sound *tsh* as in *check, chip,* and *child.*

The *ch* combination occurs also in words like *chorus* and *lichen,* where the *c* is pronounced as a *k,* and in *machine* and *gouche,* where the *c* is pronounced as an *s.* There are at least three ways of pronouncing the *ch.*

The use of *c* for the *k* sound, as in *can, scone, school, cat, cay, cuss, camp, car, chorus, lichen,* etc., has no reasonable justification. We can use the *k* instead, as is presently used in similar words like *kin, skimp, skull, king, kit, key, kitten, kiss, keg, kennel,* etc. *K* is used by the IPA and other languages to represent the *k* sound.

The use of *c* for the *s* sound also has no justification. Why should *cinder* be spelled with *c* and *sender* with an *s*? In words like *cent, cigar, civilian, cinder,* and *machine,* the letter *s* should be used in place of *c.*

There are other words where *c* is used in combination with the letter *e* or other letters to represent the *s* sound, such as *face, nice,* and *dance.* The letter *s* belongs also in those words.

The third sound that the letter *c* is used for is the *tsh* sound as in *chap, check, chip, chop, chunk, rich, match, satchel,* etc. I call it the *tsh* sound, based on the following very simple analysis.

Pronounce the word *nutshell.* Now pronounce *satchel.* Is there any difference between the *tsh* and *tch* pronunciations? I cannot detect it in my pronunciation. Most people say that there is no difference.

Here is another example. Say the word *hop*. Now add the letter *s* in front of it. It becomes *shop*. Pronounce it. Now add the letter *t* in front of it, to make it *tshop*. Say that word out loud. It sounds like you just said *chop*. The conclusion is that *tshop* and *chop* sound alike.

You can do the same exercise with the words *ship*, *tship*, and *chip*, and *shoot*, *tshoot*, and *chute*. You'll come to the same conclusion.

Oh, I am sure that some native speakers of English will argue that their pronunciation of *ch* as in *chip* does not sound exactly the same as when they pronounce *tship*. That may be true. Especially in the English language, different people pronounce words differently. The same person can pronounce the *ch* differently depending in what word it appears, what vowel is next to it. As an example, try pronouncing *chip* and *choose*. Isn't there a slight difference in the *ch* sound? The difference comes from the fact that the shaping of our mouth and lips is different when we pronounce the different vowels in those words.

A critic of the spelling change needs to take into account that presently there are at least three different ways to pronounce *ch*. That was pointed out above. The Simpel-Fonetik eliminates that frustrating spelling problem.

But one could also argue that the fewer letters, the better—why go from two letters to three by substituting *tsh* for *ch*?

Let's look at the words *ditch*, *fetch*, *stitch*, *latch*, *pitch*, *catch*, *match*, *crotch*, and *stretch*. Here is what they look like when we spell them as *ditsh*, *fetsh*, *stitsh*, *lätsh*, *pitsh*, *kätsh*, *mätsh*, *krotsh*, *stretsh*. You can see that we are not always going from two letters to three. The letter *t* already exists in those words and many others. We just change the *c* to an *s*.

Why is there a *t* in *witch* but not in *which*? They both are pronounced the same way. The same question applies to *stitch* and *rich, Dutch* and *such,* and many others.

The Simpel-Fonetik spelling does away with that dilemma. In all the above words it sounds like the *t* belongs there, so we put it there. All those *ch* and *tch* endings become *tsh.* That change amounts to a great simplification, improvement in logic, and consistency in English spelling.

In German and some other languages, the *ch* is pronounced as a strong guttural *h* sound (*hh*). The word *such* is pronounced as *suhh. Such* means *search* in German. This conflict in pronunciations between English and German and other languages will be eliminated by replacing the *ch* with *tsh.* That advantage, of course, does not matter to a person who never gets involved with a foreign language or is not interested in other people's problems with English. It matters, however, when one looks at English as being used globally by millions of foreigners.

J, j

Use *j* as a substitute for *y* in words like *yes* and *you*, which will become *jes* and *ju*, and stop using *j* for the *dsh* sound as in *Jim*, which will become *Dshim*.

These choices were made with painful awareness that there will be immediate negative reactions by many native English speakers; maybe not so much to the use of *j* in *yes*, but definitely to the use of *dsh* for the *j* as in *Jim* sound. I am hoping that my explanations that are presented here and under the discussion of the letter *Y* will help to overcome the uneasiness about the change.

The big question is: Why should one do away with the use of *j* as in *Jim*?

One reason is that in nearly all international usage, and in the International Phonetic Alphabet (IPA), the letter *j* has a different sound: the sound of *y* in *yes*. Spanish is an exception: *j* is pronounced as *h*; for example, *junta* is pronounced *hunta*.

The Esperanto language converted the use of *y* to *j*. That language uses the word *yes*, but it is spelled with the *j*, as *jes*. It seems reasonable that in the process of making changes to make English easier to learn and to use, and to be favored as a global language, we also change the present English use of *j* to conform with the prevailing use of *j* in other languages.

But another reason, the main reason, for changing the usage of *j* is that when we pronounce the words *Jim, James, jingle*, and others like them, we can hear a combination of several sounds in the pronunciation of *j*. The letter *j* in the present English spelling is being used for more than one sound. That violates the single-sound-per-letter principle of Simpel-Fonetik spelling.

The fact that *j* as in *Jim* represents at least two sounds is well demonstrated in various foreign language dictionaries, the dictionaries that show the pronunciation of English words. The dictionaries that use the IPA for showing how the letter *j* should be pronounced in words like *Jim, James,* and *jingle* use a combination of letters. There is always the letter *d*, followed by another letter or two, but the choice of those additional letters is not consistent. Sometimes a version of the letter *z* is used, which looks like the number 3. Sometimes either the letter *ž* or *š* is used. Sometimes the dictionaries use the IPA symbol that looks like this: ʃ. This symbol in other places of the same dictionary is used for the *sh* sound as in *shim, shame,* and *shingle*.

Therefore, the substitution of *dsh* for the letter *j* that is used in *Jim* is not a novel, unique, or unusual idea.

This substitution can also be explained the following way:

Let's take two words, *made* and *shirt* and put them together to become *made-shirt*. And let's substitute the *d* for the *t* so that the word becomes *made-shird*. Pronounce it as one word. Now pronounce the word *majored*. Don't the two words sound similar? In the word *made-shird*, you pronounced the *dsh* combination (the *e* is silent).

Look at the word *shim* (a small wedge-shaped item). Pronounce it. Now add the letter *d* to it, making it *dshim*. Pronounce it. Do it again a little faster. Doesn't it sound like *Jim*?

One could do the same exercise with words like *shames* and *dshames,* which sounds like *James*. Also *shingle* and *dshingle*, which sounds like *jingle*. And so on.

These examples show that the letter *j*, the way it is commonly pronounced in English, contains the *sh* sounds, or something very close to it, depending on the pronunciation skills and the dialect of the speaker. The *sh* sound is in many English words such as *shim, shame,* and *shingle* that we just used, and that is a phonetically correct usage. It would be inconsistent and in violation of the one-sound-per-letter rule to use the letter *j* for the *sh* sound—actually the *sh* plus the *d* sound.

I'll use the word *jungle* as another example to support the use of *dsh* for *j*. That word originated in India. Germans adopted it from the English and wrote it as Dschungel.

They converted the *j* to *dsh*. Well, actually to *dsch,* but the *c* does not need to be there. I think Germans will delete it from their version some day. It is bad enough to substitute three letters for *j*, but to add the *c*, a fourth letter, that is too much.

Because I am proposing to substitute three letters for the single letter *j*, the question will come up: Couldn't we use a single letter in place of the two letters *sh* to reduce the number of letters? Couldn't we consider a letter like *ž* or *š* ? Then we could write *Jim* as *Džim* or *Džim*.

My answer is that this would introduce two problems. First, we would have a new letter to deal with. Secondly, one could claim that the new letter should replace the *sh* not only in the *dsh* combination, but wherever the *sh* appears in a word. There would be the tendency to replace the *sh* in words such as *shim, dish, push,* and *shop*—they would be changed to *šim, diš, puš,* and *šop*. That, in my opinion, introduces a big disadvantage: It would change words that are presently spelled phonetically correctly, and it would complicate the proposed phonetic spelling much more than the use of three letters instead of two.

There is another argument for retaining the *sh* instead of substituting a single letter for the *sh*. Look at the word *him* and pronounce it. Now add the letter *s*. The word becomes *shim*. Pronounce it. The basic *him* sound is still there. Then why should we do away with the letter *h* when we go to *shim*? When we substitute another letter for the *sh*, we would do that. That substitution would not only change the present good phonetic spelling of many words, but it would violate the single-sound-per-letter principle.

Some people will argue that the *dsh* does not sound exactly the same as the *j* in *Jim*. It is a valid argument, because *dsh* can be pronounced differently by different people. As was pointed out above and in the discussion of the letter C, different people pronounce words differently no matter what letters are used. The Simpel-Fonetik alphabet was not derived to cover all possible variations of pronunciations. It would take more than forty letters to do that. The Simpel-Fonetik spelling strives for simplicity and for having a minimum number of letters.

In the discussion of the letter C, it was concluded that the letters *ch,* as used in *chin,* should be replaced by *tsh* to make it *tshin.* One could justify the use of *dsh* also by reasoning that if we already use *tsh,* it makes sense to use also *dsh.* The difference between the *ch* and the *j* sounds is that the *j* sound is a little softer than the *ch* sound— just compare the pronunciations of *chop* and *job.* Therefore, it is logical to use the letter *d,* the softer version of *t,* in place of *t.*

If *dsh* is substituted for *j,* then *j* becomes available for use in lieu of the letter *y* in words like *yes* and *you.* The substitution of the letter *j* for *y* is discussed next under the analysis of the letter Y.

Y, y

Not needed; used only in classical English and foreign words

In the English language, the letter y is presently used for three different sounds:

(1) In the words *my, sky, tyrant, typewriter, cycle,* and many others, *y* represents the combination of *a* and *i* sounds, *a* as in *art* and *i* as in *India,* as in the word *aisle.* Therefore, *my* could be written as *mai* and *sky* as *skai.* One would not miss the letter *y* for these uses.

(2) In the words *typical, rhythm, nymph, bicycle,* and others, the letter *y* is pronounced like the letter *i* in *India.* Therefore, the letter *y* could be replaced by *i. Typical* would then become *tipikal.* One can conclude that the letter *y* is not needed for these uses.

(3) The third sound for which the letter *y* is being used in English, the sound that is used in *yes, you,* and *canyon,* is the sound for which the IPA, the Estonian, Finnish, German, and many other languages, including Esperanto, use the letter *j.*

Should we leave the *y* for use at least in *yes* and *you* and similar sound applications? Here are some answers.

In the original Greek alphabet, the letter *y* is pronounced as *üpsilon*. In the IPA alphabet, the letter *y* is used to represent the *ü* sound. In many languages, including Estonian, Finnish, Swedish, and German, the *y* is sounded the same way as the letter *Ü, ü*. That letter appears in the name of the famous Oktoberfest town of München, Germany. If you know how to pronounce München, or have heard how the *y* in *Olympic Games* is pronounced by other than native English speakers, you know the *ü* sound.

Many languages, including the Estonian and German languages, don't use the letter *y* except when it occurs in foreign or borrowed words.

By doing away with the use of *y* for the *j* sound by substituting *j* for *y*, we will do away with a serious conflict with many other languages. We will avoid confusing the *y* with the *ü* sound. It would be a great help in the learning and usage of English by foreigners and in the globalization of the English language. Therefore, I recommend that the letter *y* be replaced by the letter *j* in words like *yes, you,* and *canyon*, writing them as *jes, ju,* and *känjon*.

Consequently, there will be no need for *y* in the new method of writing.

New Letters

In the discussion of the letter *a*, it was concluded that we need new letters for two of the sounds that are presently conveyed by the letter *a*. Those were the sounds in the words like *ant* and *fat* and in words like *ago* and *learn*. The letters *Ä, ä* and *Ö, ö* were proposed to be added to the English alphabet. Let's look at each of those letters.

Ä, ä

The letter *ä* has been around for long time. It is used in Estonian, Finnish, German, and other languages. In Estonian and Finnish, it has exactly the same sound as the *a* in English words *ant, fat, man,* and *happy*.

In the IPA, the *ä* sound is represented by an unusual letter, a combination of the letters *a* and *e* back-to-back (Æ, æ). The Danish and Norwegian languages use that letter. I don't know if it is used in any other languages.

The German language has the letter *ä* but it is pronounced slightly differently from the Estonian and Finnish *ä*. It sounds almost like a quick and sloppy pronunciation of *ae*. Perhaps for that reason, in Germany the letter *ä* is sometimes replaced by the letters *ae*.

But that substitution cannot be done in a truly phonetic, only one-sound-per-letter spelling system, which is considered here. The *ae* would be sounded out as *a* and *e*, and it would not sound like *ä*.

The Swedes have the letter *ä*, and in most cases they pronounce it also as the *a* in *ant*, but they have some variations in sounding that letter, depending where it appears in the word.

Back in the fifties when we had no computers, my parents did have a problem with the letter *ä*—the letter *ä* was missing on most American typewriters. They had to type the letter *a* and add the dots by hand. But now, in the age of computers and word processors, a simple additional keystroke, or holding down additional keys, makes the letter *ä* immediately available. A good solution is to assign the letter *ä*, and also *ö*, to the keyboard's Function keys. Of course, once the letter *ä* is accepted in the English language, it will become an integral part of the keyboards of English-speaking countries.

The keyboards of German, Finnish, Estonian, and other languages already include the letters *ä* and *ö*.

In my opinion, the adding of the dots to the letter *a* is simpler than learning to write a totally new letter, such as *Æ, æ*.

Let's add the letter *Ä, ä* to the English alphabet.

Ö, ö

Because we chose the *a* as in *art* sound for the letter *a*, and because we are following the one-sound-per-letter rule, we need a letter to replace the sound that is presently conveyed by the letter *a* in words *ago, another, awhile,* and *alike*.

That replacement letter could also be used for the same, but perhaps a little longer sound, that is in *word, occurs, turn, stir, fir, learn,* and *her*.

Please note how in the above words different vowels in combination with the letter *r* can call for that special sound. There appears to be no rule as to when it occurs. One needs to learn how to pronounce each word. For example, the words *cord* and *word* differ only by the first letter, yet they are pronounced quite differently. *Cord* has the *o* sound, but *word* has the sound for which the Estonian, Finnish, German, and other languages use the letter *ö*.

The name of the country that the English speakers call Austria is Österreich. The famous town in Germany that has a huge, beautiful cathedral is named Köln, but we call it Cologne. I guess we had to use different names for those places because we did not have the letter *ö*, and we did not know how to pronounce it.

There are many other examples where the Brits and Americans had to distort the name of some place or person because the letter *ö* was not part of the alphabet.

There are two IPA letters that are also used to represent the *ö* sounds. For the shorter of the two, the sound of *a* in *ago*, the IPA uses a symbol (called *schwa*) that looks like the letter *e* upside down. It is not readily available on my computer.

For the longer version, as in *turn*, I have seen the use of two of those upside down *e* symbols. But I have seen also a symbol that looks like the letter *o* with a slash through it (Ø, ø). That symbol is used as a letter in the Danish and Norwegian languages.

In the German language, and also in English, the letter *ö* is sometimes substituted by the letters *o* and *e*. For example, the name *Röntgen*, the discoverer of X-rays, is spelled in the College Dictionary as *Roentgen*.

As I mentioned in the discussion of the letter *Ä*, we are basing our selection of letters on one sound per letter, and as in the Estonian language, we enunciate each letter. Therefore, the use of *oe* for *ö* will not work. It won't sound right.

The IPA letter that is an upside down *e* is a strange new letter that is not easily available on keyboards and is hard to get used to in handwriting. I don't even know what its capital letter version looks like. Therefore, I don't favor it for the *ö* sound.

The other IPA letter, the one that looks like an *o* with a slash through it (*ø*), can be confused with the number zero. Zero is sometimes written with a slash to distinguish it from the letter *o*.

The letter *ö* is readily available on computers and word processors. It is easy to use in handwriting, and it has served well in many other languages.

It's about time we include the letter *ö* in the English alphabet.

New Alphabet

Let's review how the alphabet will be affected by the Simpel-Fonetik writing method:

1. These letters will be used as they are now:
   B D F K L M N P V Z
2. These letters will have one sound only:
   A E G H I J O R S T U W
3. These letters will not be needed:
   C Q X Y
4. These letters need to be added to the alphabet:
   Ä Ö
5. The addition of these letters is optional:
   Ü Ő

The letter *Ü* is not needed for the phonetic spelling of English. But it is needed for dealing with other important languages, such as German, just like other languages use English letters for dealing with English names and expressions. We need to add it to the alphabet sooner or later, especially if we expect English to be used worldwide.

The letter *Õ*—the letter *O* with a tilde (a wavy dash) above it—is used in the Estonian language to represent a sound between the *ä* and the *ö* sounds when one considers the positioning of the lips and the tongue in producing speech sounds. It sounds somewhat like the *o* in the British dialect-like pronunciation of *low*. Therefore, the letter *õ* could be used to represent that sound if and when needed. But the proposed phonetic spelling of English can get by without it.

As far as the four unneeded letters of the present alphabet are concerned, I think we should keep them in the alphabet because we need to deal with them for a long time to come. New York is not going to change its name and neither will Chicago—we need to be able to write them. Perhaps we should use parentheses or asterisks to indicate that those letters are not used in the phonetic writing method.

The two new letters, *ä* and *ö*, will need to be placed someplace into the alphabet. The question is, where?

There are several choices.

One choice is to place the *ä* right behind the *a* and the *ö* behind the *o*. This is logical because the sounds are written almost alike—we just added two dots—and the dotted sound is close to the undotted sound. The alphabet would be as follows:

AÄBCDEFGHIJKLMNOÖPQRSTUVWXYZ

The second choice is to place the new sounds at the end of the alphabet. This may be considered to have the advantage that existing filing systems will not be disturbed by inserting new letters between existing letters.

One of the problems with the placement of the new letters at the end may be that many organizations whose names begin with the letter *A,* but with the phonetic alphabet will convert to *Ä,* will find themselves at the end of all files and telephone listings. I don't think that the *Är Fors* will put up with being at the end while the *Armi* enjoys being way up front.

The Germans, in their dictionaries, intermingle the Ä with the A and the Ö with the letter O. There are no separate listings for Ä or Ö. To look up a word starting with the letter Ä you look under A. For the order of listing they treat Ä as if it were A. Same with the letter Ö. In my opinion, in German language the letters *ä* and *ö* just don't get a fair treatment, as if they don't qualify to be considered as separate and equal letters.

Is it worth considering the German way of treating *ä* and *ö* for our alphabet?

I don't think so. My choice is the first choice listed above, placing the Ä close to A, Ö close to O.

We can have two alphabets:

The basic alphabet, consisting of twenty-four letters used in the phonetic English.

A Ä B D E F G H I J K L M N O Ö P R S T U V W Z

The expanded alphabet, consisting of twenty-eight letters. The extra letters are marked with an asterisk (*).

A Ä B C* D E F G H I J K L M N O Ö P Q* R S T U V W X* Y* Z

The sounds for reciting the alphabet need to be revised to conform with the change to a single sound per letter. For example, one should not recite the letter *a* as in *may,* or the letter *i* as in *I,* or the letter *e* as in *me,* when they are no longer used for those sounds.

Here is how the new, expanded alphabet could be recited:

Aa, ää, bee, tse, dee, ee, ef, gee, haa, ii, jot, kaa, el, em, en, oo, öö, pee, kjuu, er, es, tee, uu, vee, wee, eks, wai, zii.

The pronunciation is shown in Simpel-Fonetik writing. I hesitated to use it because I have not yet completed the description of the Simpel-Fonetik writing. But the other choice was to use the strange International Phonetic Alphabet letters. The use of Simpel-Fonetik was much easier.

If, at this stage, you have problems in reading and pronouncing the letters the way they are shown, I suggest you give up for now and come back to it later, after learning in the following chapters how groups of letters and words that are written in Simpel-Fonetik are enunciated—properly sounded out.

International Alphabet

The International Radiotelephony Spelling Alphabet, also known as the NATO Phonetic Alphabet, is used in communications all over the world by many organizations, including the International Civil Aviation Organization (ICAO), the International Telecommunication Union (ITU), the North Atlantic Treaty Organization (NATO), the Federal Aviation Administration (FAA), and the American National Standards Institute (ANSI).

Here is the alphabet and the call, or code, words for each letter:

A — Alfa	B — Bravo	C — Charlie
D — Delta	E — Echo	F — Foxtrot
G — Golf	H — Hotel	I — India
J — Juliet	K — Kilo	L — Lima
M — Mike	N — November	O — Oscar
P — Papa	Q — Quebec	R — Romeo
S — Sierra	T — Tango	U — Uniform
V — Victor	W — Whiskey	X — X-ray
Y — Yankee	Z — Zulu	

The international alphabet is identical to the expanded alphabet proposed for the Simpel-Fonetik method of writing, with the exception that the version used by native English speakers does not include the letters *Ä, Ö,* and *Ü.*

The countries in which the letters *Ä, Ö,* and *Ü* are in everyday use have added those letters to the international alphabet for their use. Here is what the Germans have added:

Ä — Ärger (anger) Ö — Öse (grommet)
Ü — Übel (evil)

It is important to notice that in the international alphabet, all letters have the same sounds, or pronunciations, as established for the Simpel-Fonetik spelling. The letter *e* has the sound as in *echo,* the letter *i* as in *India,* the letter *g* as in *golf,* and so on.

Even the letter *a* in the international alphabet comes out sounding like the *a* in the Simpel-Fonetik when *alfa* is pronounced as it is pronounced in Greece, where the word comes from. Most users of the international alphabet pronounce both *a*'s in *alfa* the same way, as the *a* in *art.* Only Americans and some other native English speakers tend to change the pronunciation of the first *a* in *alfa* to an *ä,* pronouncing the word as *älfa.*

The letter *j* also tends to be pronounced in two ways. People who are not used to speaking English tend to pronounce the *J* in *Juliet* as the sound of *y* in *you.* That is how it is pronounced in many European languages, and that is the sound given to *j* in the International Phonetic Alphabet. That is the sound chosen for *j* in the Simpel-Fonetik alphabet. But most English speakers tend to pronounce the *J* in *Juliet* as in *Jim.*

The four letters C, Q, X, and Y, have pronunciations based on the present English spelling and pronunciations. But those letters are not used for the Simpel-Fonetik writing, so it does not matter.

It is interesting to note that in the international alphabet the word *alfa* is spelled with *f* rather than with *ph*. The American dictionaries still use the *ph* in *alpha*. The Simpel-Fonetik spelling agrees with the international alphabet also in substituting *f* for *ph*.

The letters *Ä* and *Ö*, and also the letter *Ü*, in my opinion, will need to be added to the international alphabet used by the Americans and the Brits. With that addition, the Simpel-Fonetik alphabet and the international alphabet will be one and the same, totally compatible with each other.

The international alphabet was intended for global use. The Simpel-Fonetik writing method was developed with the visualization of English as a global language. That is why the two match so well.

Matching Letters to Sounds

Double Letters

In the Estonian, Finnish, German, and many other languages, two of the same letters are used to represent a longer vowel or a stronger consonant.

This is not a strange concept in the English language.

Let's look at some examples:

For has the short vowel *o*, and *floor* is pronounced with a long *o* sound.
Dog has the short vowel *o*, and *door* is pronounced with a long *o* sound.
Sin has the weaker consonant *n*, and *sinner* has a stronger or longer *n*.
Pal has the weaker consonant *l*, and *pallet* has a stronger or longer *l*.

But I am running out of these logical samples. I find more and more samples that are illogical and inconsistent.

For example, the long version of *fit* should be *fiit*, but it is not. It is *feet*. Instead of two *i*'s, there are two *e*'s.

But there is also the word *feat*, pronounced exactly like *feet*, where the vowels *e* and *a* are used to give the long *i* sound. So it seems that you use either *ee* or *ea* to represent the long *i* sound.

For example: *Lip – leap, rip – reap, kip – keep, sit – seat, sip – seep, dip – deep.*

But there is also the word *fete* that has the long *i* sound. And the words *field, fiend, lien,* and many others where the letters *ie* are used for the long *i* sound.

It turns out that a variety of letters are used for the long *i* sound.

And for the long *o* sound, besides the *oo* as in *door,* one can also use *augh* as in *caught,* or *ough* as in *thought,* or *ou* as in *mourn,* or *oa* as in *soar,* or an *o* before and an *e* after the *r,* as in *sore,* and various other combinations of letters.

Someone learning English would think that the word *loot* is the long-sounding version of *lot.* But the *o* sound does not exist in either of those words. *Loot* has the long *u* sound and *lot* is usually pronounced as if it had an *a* as in *art* in it.

The *double o (oo)* in present English can be pronounced in at least four ways. Compare the pronunciations of the following words: *floor, foot, pool, zoology.*

This is why the students learning English must learn how to spell and pronounce each word separately and remember exactly which combination of letters applies to each word. There is no rule.

It should be clear to all of us that these spelling problems beg to be corrected. There needs to be some law and order, logic and consistency, in the English spelling.

We have established one rule already—the rule of one sound per letter. We need just one more rule for the Simpel-Fonetik spelling method.

Here is the second rule:

For longer vowels and stronger consonants, use double letters—just add another letter with the same sound.

This rule is simple to use for new words, but when converting existing words to Simpel-Fonetik writing, often it is difficult to decide if there should be one or two letters. That problem is caused by the fact that the present English spelling often leaves the pronunciation open for interpretation. For example, in *good-bye,* the *u* sound expressed with the two *o*'s is pronounced as if there were only one *u.* In the word *tool,* however, it is clear that there is a long *u* sound.

Another example is the word *bean.* It clearly has a long *i* sound. It would be written *biin.* But the word *been,* even though it has two *e*'s, implying a long vowel sound, is usually pronounced as *bin.*

There are many other words like that. Therefore, the use of double letters in present spelling cannot be used to guide in deciding if double letters should also be used in Simpel-Fonetik spelling. The present spellings can mislead you.

I have found that the best way to determine if double letters should be used is to write the word down phonetically, in Simpel-Fonetik, using only one letter at first. Then read and pronounce the word as it is written. If the word sounds acceptable, close enough, and does not sound like it would conflict with another word, leave it that way. If, however, it sounds like the vowel or consonant is too short, add the other letter.

As an example, let's look at the word *peace.* You could write it first as *pis.* But right away you realize that it could be pronounced as *piss.* So there is no question that *peace* should be written as *piis.*

The word *you* in some usage sounds like it has two *u*'s. But for most usage, the sound of *ju* will be acceptable. Using two *u*'s, as in *hau ar juu,* puts too much emphasis on the word *you.* That is avoided in *hau ar ju.*

But the word *youth*, when written as *juth*, just does not sound right with the short *u*. It sounds better with the second *u*, as in *juuth*.

And don't be fooled by words like *fall*, where a single letter is used for a long sound and double letters are used for a regular-length sound. It would be converted to phonetic spelling as *fool* (don't pronounce it as *fuul*).

Hissing Sounds

In the basic Estonian language, there are no *c, ch, sh,* or *z* sounds. There is only the plain *s* sound. That situation has helped to make the language more tonal, more suitable for singing, and easier to enunciate and understand words. This is especially appreciated by people with poor hearing. And when you listen to the Estonian language, it is easier on the ears than, for example, the Russian language, which has a multitude of *sh* sounds, or the German language, which has the guttural *ch* sounds as in *Achtung* (attention) or *nichts* (nothing). The German word *Schinken* (ham) is plain *sink* in Estonian, pronounced exactly as the phonetically correct English word *sink*.

Did you know that the Hawaiian language has no *s* sound at all, nor the *r* sound?

The English language has quite a few of the so-called hissing sounds, in addition to the letter *s*, but they are not as "throat-clearing" as the German *ch*.

Probably the mildest of those sounds is the *z* sound as in *zipper* and *zebra*. The sound is somewhat close to the *s* sound, but not close enough to be replaced by *s*. And there is no *h* component in the pronunciation of *z*. The letter *z* is in the IPA, and in English it is pronounced exactly as the IPA's *z*. All considered, the letter *z* deserves to be included for use in the Simpel-Fonetik English writing.

The main use of the letter *z* is in words like *zinc, zipper,* and *zone.* But the letter *z* is sometimes also used in phonetic spellings of words like *garage, vision,* and *pleasure.* In some dictionaries the pronunciations for those words are shown with the IPA symbol that looks like the old Gothic *z*, somewhat similar to number 3. It is not a letter in common use. The letters *zh* are sometimes used in place of it.

Let's look at the word *garage* as an example of some of the complications that may rise in converting a word, especially a word with multiple pronunciations, to Simpel-Fonetik spelling.

In my Microsoft Encarta Dictionary, the pronunciation of *garage* is shown with *zh*, as *göraazh* (I use an *ö* in place of the upside down *e*). The dictionary also shows an alternate pronunciation as *göraaj*.

My Estonian-English dictionary, which is based on British English, shows pronunciation of *garage* as *gäraazh* and an alternate pronunciation as *gäridzh*. That, of course, is based on the similarity of *garage* with words like *carriage, adage, manage,* etc., which all have a similar-sounding ending.

The Estonian word for *garage* is spelled with a special letter *ž* (a *z* with a small *v* or a checkmark over it, used for foreign words), as *garaaž*. This is the official spelling, but many people are converting to the use of either *zh* or *sh* in place of the *ž*. That appears to be caused by two reasons: (1) the use of *ž*, an additional, strange letter, just appears too fancy or pedantic, and (2) the letter *ž* is not readily available on keyboards.

With this cursorily described research background, I contemplated what should be used for the word *garage* in Simpel-Fonetik spelling.

Based on the guidance in college dictionaries, the use of *zh* looked most favorable until I tried to pronounce the *zh* phonetically. I tried to say *z* as in *zinc*, quickly followed by *h* as in *hotel*, but when I added that combination sound to the ending of *garage*, as *garaazh*, it was not only difficult to say out loud, but it did not sound right.

Then I tried to use the *sh* ending in place of the *zh*. I had no problems with it, and the word sounded fine to me.

I also tried Encarta's alternate pronunciation based on the use of *j* at the end, indicating a *dsh* or *dzh* sound. That also sounded okay.

Because people pronounce the word *garage* in so many ways, and the dictionaries have not set a standard for it, I concluded that for Simpel-Fonetik, the best spelling would be as *garaash*. It is the simplest version. The new learners of English will appreciate it.

The same spelling could be applied also to *vision—vishön* and to *pleasure—pleshör*.

Under the discussion of the letter *C*, it was concluded that the *ch* should be replaced by *tsh*. But please note that *ch* is not used consistently. Look at the following words:

cache   *machine*   *lichen*   *chemical*   *choir*

We can't use the *tsh* substitution in the above words. They require different letters. Here is how they would be written in Simpel-Fonetik:

käsh   *mäshiin*   *laiken*   *kemikal*   *kwair*

The point is that *ch* is used for various sounds. When we convert a word that has a *ch* in it to the phonetic spelling, we must recognize what sound the *ch* represents. Most of the time it is the *tsh* sound, but it can also be the *sh* or the *k* sound, or even some other sound.

Additional hissing sounds in the English language are produced by the letters *c, g, h, j, s,* and *t,* in different combinations and associations with other letters.

The letter *g* is presently used for two sounds. One is for the sound of *g* as in *go* and *golf,* and that is how *g* will be used in Simpel-Fonetik. The second use of *g* is for the sound of *j* as in *jeans.* The word *genes* is an example of this second use. Please note that the two words *jeans* and *genes* are pronounced identically; in speaking, one cannot tell the difference between the two. Because this second use of *g* is identical to the use of *j,* there is no need to discuss it separately. Whatever was discussed under *J, j* applies also to the second use of *g.* Just like *j,* the letter *g* will be replaced by *dsh.*

The use of letters like *j* and *g* to represent the *sh* and *dsh* sounds has served nicely to hide the fact that there are many, perhaps too many, hissing sounds in the English language. When you see *Jim, George,* or *June* in print, the words look more pleasing than the true-sound representations *Dshim, Dshordsh,* and *Dshun.* The conversion to the use of the *dsh* and *tsh* will reveal the widespread use of hissing sounds in the English language.

I feel that it needs to be revealed. Maybe that will help to avoid adding even more words with hissing sounds.

Let's review the recommendations and conclusions pertaining to the *s, sh, dsh, and tsh* sounds.

1. Replace all *s*-sounding *c*'s with *s.*
   Examples: *center* becomes *senter, nice* becomes *nais.*
2. Replace all *sh*-sounding *s*'s, *ch*'s, and *ge*'s with *sh.*
   Examples: *sugar* becomes *shugar, pleasure* becomes *pleshör, machine* becomes *mäshiin, garage* becomes *garaash.*

3. Replace all *sh*-sounding combinations of various letters, such as *ti, ss, ce, sc,* and others with *sh.*

   Examples: *nation* becomes *neishon, tissue* becomes *tishu, ocean* becomes *oushan, conscience* becomes *kanshens.*

4. Replace all *dsh*-sounding *j*'s with *dsh.*

   Examples: *jet* becomes *dshet, jog* becomes *dshog.*

5. Replace all *dsh*-sounding *g*'s with *dsh.*

   Examples: *gender* becomes *dshender, binge* becomes *bindsh.*

6. Replace all *tsh*-sounding *ch*'s with *tsh.*

   Examples: *chin* becomes *tshin, kitchen* becomes *kitshen.*

In summary, the Simpel-Fonetik does away with the use of the letters *c, g,* and *j* for the hissing sounds. It does away with the use of *ti, ss, ce, sc,* and many other combinations of letters for the *sh* sound.

The spelling of the hissing sounds is simplified to the point that there is only the basic letter *s,* modified by *h* to represent the *sh* sound, and further modified by either *d* or *t* to represent the *dsh* or *tsh* sounds. The letter *s,* in combinations with *h, d,* and *t* takes care of all the hissing sounds in the English language, except where the letter *z* is needed. The letter *z* will be used as it is now.

Diphthongs AI, EI, AU, OI, OU, ÖU, EÖ, and IÖ

In the present English language, there are many combinations of vowels used in inconsistent and irregular ways to represent various sounds. The Simpel-Fonetik spelling brings order and logic to the use of diphthongs, vowel combinations like *au* and *ou*, and various other combinations of letters that represent different diphthong sounds. Let's look at the most commonly used diphthongs and see how they will be used in various Simpel-Fonetik words.

AI

In the present English writing, there is at least one word that makes phonetically correct use of *ai*, and that is the word *aisle*. The word means a passageway between seats or between shelves of goods. In that word the letters *a* and *i* are pronounced as they should be and as they will be in Simpel-Fonetik.

Oh yes, there is a problem with the rest of the spelling of *aisle*—the *s* and *e* are silent. We can't have that in Simpel-Fonetik. The word will be spelled as *ail*.

But now you know how the *ai* should be used and pronounced.

It is too bad that this use of *ai* was not established for the rest of the words where that sound appears in the present English spelling. Instead, we have the following other combinations of letters for the *ai* sound, and these are just a few samples:

time	*fine*	*mine*
my	*dry*	*spy*
stye	*dye*	*lye*
sign	*align*	*benign*
rice	*twice*	*mice*
icon	*item*	*ire*

Notice that sometimes *y* is used alone, sometimes *y* and *e* are used together, sometimes *i* is used alone, as in *icon* and *item*, but sometimes an *e* needs to be added as in *time, fine,* and *mine.* All these different spellings are used to produce the *ai* sound.

In the Simpel-Fonetik method there is only one way to write the *ai* sound. Below are the above words re-written:

taim	*fain*	*main*
mai	*drai*	*spai*
stai	*dai*	*lai*
sain	*ölain*	*binain*
rais	*twais*	*mais*
aikon	*aitem*	*aier*

EI

There are several examples where the letters *ei* are used phonetically, as they would be in Simpel-Fonetik.

veil   *feign*   *sleigh*

The present English pronunciation of the *ei* in the above words should serve as a guide for pronouncing *ei* in the proposed new spellings. But again, there are some silent letters involved. The words will be spelled as follows in Simpel-Fonetik:

veil   *fein*   *slei*

Here are some samples of words where different combinations of letters are used for the *ei* sound. Note that there are *a* and *e* combinations, *ay* and *ai* used for the *ei* sound.

make	sane	frame	great
play	pray	foray	
rain	saint	campaign	

The above words will be spelled as follows in Simpel-Fonetik:

meik	sein	freim	greit
plei	prei	forei	
rein	seint	kämpein	

AU

The letters *au* in the present English writing usually have the phonetic sound of *oo*, or double *o*. Examples:

taut   *caught*   *plausible*

In Simpel-Fonetik those words are spelled as follows:

toot	*koot*	*ploosibl*

The Simpel-Fonetik sound *au* is found in present spelling mainly in words that use the *ou* and the *ow* combinations. Examples:

sound	*house*	*loud*
cow	*frown*	*crowd*

Both of these combinations are replaced in Simpel-Fonetik by *au*, as follows:

saund	*haus*	*laud*
kau	*fraun*	*kraud*

OI

The following words are examples of phonetically correct use of the diphthong *oi*. These words require no change:

heroin	*groin*	*loin*	*moist*
ointment	*point*	*spoil*	*toilet*

In the following words, the letter *y* is presently used in place of *i*:

annoy	*boy*	*convoy*	*destroy*	*royal*	*toy*

In Simpel-Fonetik they will be spelled with the letter *i*, as follows:

annoi	*boi*	*konvoi*	*destroi*	*roial*	*toi*

OU

The sound *ou* can be heard more in the American than the British pronunciations. In the present spelling, it appears in several combinations of letters. Here are some samples:

oak	*boat*	*roast*
dope	*yoke*	*note*
ghost	*most*	*host*
mow	*low*	*tow*
sew		

In Simpel-Fonetik, all these different versions would be changed to a consistent, phonetically logical spelling as follows:

ouk	*bout*	*roust*
doup	*jouk*	*nout*
goust	*moust*	*houst*
mou	*lou*	*tou*
sou		

ÖU

To show the British pronunciation of the above words, one needs to substitute the diphthong *öu* in place of *ou*. Then *oak* becomes *öuk*, *boat* changes to *böut*, and so on.

This is one of the many cases of multiple pronunciations in the English language. When converting to phonetic spelling, one needs to decide which pronunciation to choose. I favor the *ou* version for these reasons: (1) the letter *o* is used in the present spelling, and (2) in other languages, the letter *o* is more popular than the letter *ö*.

Spanish, for example, does not have the letter *ö*. In trying to simplify the use of English for global use, one must consider such matters.

EÖ

Foreign language dictionaries that are based on British English use the diphthong *eö* (I am using the letter *ö* in place of the IPA letter that looks like an upside down *e*) for showing the pronunciation of words like *chair, bare, square, fair,* and *various*. They show those words pronounced as *tsheö, beö, skweö, feö,* and *veöriös*.

American dictionaries do not support that pronunciation. The *Random House College Dictionary* uses the single letter *â* (*a* with an inverted v over it) to show how those words should be pronounced. It shows *chair* pronounced as *châr*. The use of a single letter means that there is no diphthong involved.

The pronunciation guide in that dictionary uses *dâre* as the example for the use of the letter *â*. Therefore, wherever the letter *â* appears, you pronounce it the way you pronounce *dare*. This pronunciation guidance accommodates variations in pronunciation.

I have noticed that especially the non-native speakers of English, both in the United States and in Europe, are deviating from the British pronunciation more and more. They tend to pronounce the above words in a way that recognizes the existence of the letter *a*, pronounced as *ä*, in those words. And they do include the *r* sound in the pronunciations.

I, personally, favor that trend, mainly because it shows that people are paying attention to letters in a word. That is a good trend. Therefore, I favor minimizing the use of the diphthong *eö*. The words *chair, bare, square, fair,* and *various* would be spelled in Simpel-Fonetik as *tshär, bär, skwär, fär,* and *väriös*.

IÖ

This is another diphthong that is used mostly in the British pronunciations. It applies to words like *ear, fear, rear, leer,* and *peer*. They could be converted to *iö, fiö, riö, liö* and *piö*, based on pronunciation guidance in some foreign language dictionaries.

But my college dictionary shows those words pronounced as in the first letter of the word *even*, or as the *ee* in *bee*, and as the letters *ea* and *ee* in many other words such as *beat, leak, feet,* and *meet*. In Simpel-Fonetik that would call for the use of two *i*'s (*ii*) to represent the long *i* sound. And the American dictionaries show the letter *r*.

I prefer the American pronunciation because it is easier, more natural, especially for foreigners to use. The above words should be converted to *iir, fiir, riir, liir,* and *piir*.

The TH Sound

In the International Phonetic Alphabet the *th* sound, as in *this*, *that*, *neither*, and *math*, is represented by a symbol that looks like an O with a dash through the middle of it. It is not a letter in the Latin alphabet.

The *th* sound is unique to the English language. I know that Estonians, Germans, Finns—they all have problems pronouncing it. The way they tend to pronounce it, the word *this* sounds more like *tis*, or when they really try hard, it may sound like *sis*. Especially for an older person, it may take years of practice to get a passing mark in pronouncing the *th*.

So what happens in the meantime? The learners pronounce it as *t* and *h* spoken one after another. Take the word *hem*, add the letter *t* in front of it. Now sound out the *hem* word with the *t* in front of it—no, don't convert it to the *th* sound—and that's how they pronounce *them*.

That's how Germans pronounce it, because they do have the *th* combination in some of their words. But the Estonians see that letter combination only in foreign words. Their word for *theater* is spelled as *teater*, without the *h*.

I feel that the best solution is to leave the *th* as is. Different people will pronounce it differently anyway. Why worry about it? So what if it eventually evolves into a slightly different pronunciation, sounds less like a lisp, closer to what foreigners can also cope with. Besides, "no change" should be easier to accept than some new letter.

The R Sound

I remember the time when I was in the American military and had to answer the telephone in what the military called the orderly room. I was quite proficient in English—I had managed to learn to say words with the *th* pretty well already—but I had a terrible time with the American *r*. In Estonian, the *r* is pronounced with the tip of the tongue, giving it more of a trill. I just could not pronounce *orderly room* they way others did. It sounded so foreign. I practiced on a tape recorder to improve my pronunciation, but my progress was very slow.

From my personal experience, I can say that it does not matter how the Americans or Brits or other native English speakers pronounce the *r*, we just have to accept that there will be differences in pronunciation.

The Brits, more than the Americans, tend to leave the *r* totally out in words like *are, art, far, near, large, pork,* and so on.
And so do the Chinese, or they substitute the letter *l* in place of *r*. They have a really hard time pronouncing the *r*.

How should we deal with that silent, or nearly silent, *r* in the conversion to Simpel-Fonetik writing?

It appears to me that the marginal, hard-to-decide words need to be evaluated individually, based on what is in practice in other languages, what makes the word easier to understand, and what may make it sound better. In words like *art*, which is also used in other languages with the *r* in it, it is best to leave the *r* in place. In most cases, the *r* needs to be left in place to keep the word easily recognizable even after the conversion.

The teachers of English, be they in America, Great Britain, or some other country, will perhaps end up explaining to their students the pronunciation of *r* in a way similar to this:

> In America and England, the original residents usually pronounce the *r* with the middle of the tongue against the palate, with hardly any trill to it. But in both countries, there are now so many newcomers, millions of Mexicans in California alone, who pronounce the *r* the best they can, with the *r* usually ending up with more of a trill sound, as in Spanish and other European languages.
>
> In the English language there are many words where the letter *r* is not pronounced at all, or hardly at all. For example: *secure, sever, premier, here, matter, swear,* and *weather.* Foreigners tend to put an *r* sound even into those words.
>
> In the use of the new Simpel-Fonetik English, you won't have the problem of deciding when to pronounce the *r*. Whenever you see an *r*, you pronounce it. Just like the Mexicans in California, you also do the best you can.

Converting Words to Phonetic Spelling

Words with Double Meanings

In the present way of spelling English, there are words with double meanings that are *spelled the same way but are pronounced differently*, depending on what they mean. The examples mentioned before were *read, wind,* and *lead.* Additional examples are *live, bow, bass,* and *resume.*

The phonetic alphabet and spelling will correct that problem. The words will be spelled as they sound. For example, when the word *wind* refers to weather, it will be spelled just as it is now. When it refers to winding a clock, the word will be spelled *waind.* The word *lead,* when it refers to guiding, or leading the way, will be spelled *liid.* When it refers to the black stuff inside the pencil, it will be spelled *led.*

Now let's look at the words with two or more meanings that are *spelled differently but are pronounced the same way.* There are many such words in the English language. We already looked at a few in the "Problems" chapter. Here are some more examples:

Ball – bawl, bare – bear, bread – bred, buy – by, cue – queue, days – daze, deer – dear, dew – do, die – dye, doe – dough – do

(...re), *fair – fare, flower – flour, for – four, foul – fowl, fur – fir, grate – great, hall – haul, hay – hey, heal – heel, hole – whole, hour – our, idle – idol, knight – night, know – no, leak – leek, lie – lye, maid – made, male – mail, might – mite, mind – mined, mold – mould, morning – mourning, new – knew – gnu, not – nut – knot, nun – none, oar – ore – or, pair – pear – pare, pane – pain, pause – paws, peace – piece, peak – peek, peal – peel, pier – peer, plain – plane, poll – pole, pomp – pump, poor – pour, pray – prey, principal – principle, quay – key, rap – wrap, reign – rein – rain, read – reed, rest – wrest, right – rite – write, ring – wring, role – roll, rut – rot, scene – seen, scent – cent – sent, sea – see, seam – seem, some – sum, son – sun, sow – so – sew, steal – steel, straight – strait, tail – tale, there – their – they're, tide – tied, toe – tow, urn – earn, vain – vein, vice – vise, waist – waste, wait – weight, weak – week, wine – whine, witch – which, wood – would.*

When any one of the above words is spoken, there can be two or three interpretations of the word. But in the present English, when they are spelled out, written down, one can tell which of the meanings applies.

The phonetic alphabet and spelling eliminates the multiple versions of spelling. For example, the word *eight* will be spelled *eit*. The silent *g* and *h* are no longer written out. And the word *ate*, because it is pronounced exactly like *eight*, will also be spelled as *eit*. As a consequence, when you use the phonetic alphabet, it does not matter if you speak or write these multiple-meaning words; you still don't know which meaning applies.

Just as in the present English, when reading the words such as *wind* and *lead*, the meanings of the words in the above list, when written phonetically, will have to become clear from the subject under discussion, from the context, or from other clarifying words.

There are words with multiple meanings in all languages. In some languages more than in others. The English language has a multitude of them. For example, the word *call* can mean many things. We add another word to help clarify the meaning. We say *call up, call off,* or *call on*—in each case there is a totally different meaning associated with the word *call*.

Many of the double-meaning problems can be corrected in the process of converting to the Simpel-Fonetik spelling method. For example, the word *idle* could be converted to *aidl,* whereas the word *idol* could be converted to *aidol*. After the conversion, the previously silent *o* will be sounded out. That will distinguish the two meanings, both in speaking and in writing.

A similar improvement could take place in the conversion of the identically pronounced words *son* and *sun*. In the Simpel-Fonetik spelling, *sun* would be converted to *san*. The spelling of the word *son* could remain the same as it is now. Some people, especially foreign students, would tend to pronounce the word slightly differently from the present pronunciation; they would give *son* more of the *o* sound. That pronunciation would be similar to the German word *Sohn,* meaning *son*. It would also sound almost like the same word in Dutch and some other languages. With this change we would not only eliminate a double-meaning problem, but we would also support the idea of commonality among languages.

Let's look at the words *their* and *there* as another example of two similarly spoken but differently written words. In Simpel-Fonetik, both words could be spelled as *thär,* because that is how they are usually pronounced. But then the two words would be identical not only in speaking, but also in writing. A better solution is to change *there* to *thär,* but leave the word *their* as it is spelled now.

That would distinguish the two words not only in writing, but also in speaking when each letter is properly pronounced.

When the word *they* is converted to phonetic spelling, it becomes *thei*. Then the possessive form, *their,* is obtained by simply adding the letter *r*. But in the present spelling, the letter *y* in *they* needs to be changed to *i* before adding the *r* to become *their*. This switching of letters complicates spelling. Unfortunately, it is a well-established practice in the present spelling, especially in the use of suffixes.

Prefixes and Suffixes

Let's look at the prefixes, the first syllables, of the following words:

*des*cend   *dis*cern   *dys*function

They are pronounced the same way, yet they are spelled differently.

In Simpel-Fonetik, these words will be spelled as

*dis*end   *dis*örn   *dis*fankshon

There is no more guessing, pondering, looking up in the dictionary to find out if the first syllable should be *des, dis,* or *dys.* The vowel has the *i* sound, so you write *i.* This simplification applies to many other words that have similar first syllables.

Now let's look at some suffixes:

move – mov*ing*   hoe – hoe*ing*   tie – ty*ing*   ready – readi*ly*
  lady – ladie*s*   memo – memo*s*   potato – potato*es*

Notice that in the present spelling, the *e* at the end of *move* is deleted, but the *e* at the end of *hoe* is not. In the word *tie*, the *ie* changes to a *y*. In *ready* the *y* changes to an *i*, but in *lady* the *y* changes to an *ie*. The plural form of *memo* is obtained by adding the suffix *s,* but for the plural of *potato* an *s* is not enough—an *e* also needs to be added.

Here are the same words in phonetic spelling.

muuv – muuv*ing*   hou – hou*ing*   tai – tai*ing*   redi – redi*li*
  leidi – leidi*s*   memo – memo*s*   poteito – poteito*s*

Note that the addition of the suffix does not change the basic word. The sensless—oops, I misspelled; there is a silent *e* in sens*e*less— and confusing complications of the present spelling are eliminated by the Simpel-Fonetik spelling.

Words that Do Not Change

There are many words in the English language that are already written in a phonetically correct or acceptable way. They follow the basic phonetic writing rules that are used in Estonian, Finnish, German, Spanish, Portuguese, and other phonetic or almost-phonetic languages. Here are some samples:

Arsenal, arson, art, artist, bar, barn, barter, bed, beg, belt, bend, bent, best, bet, bib, bid, big, bin, blend, blink, boil, bravo, brim, bring, brink, broil, bush, dark, dart, deliver, delta, den, denim, dent, dentist, desk, didn't, dig, dip, disk, dispel, distend, distill, distort, dog, dogma, dollar, dominant, domino, don't, drama, drink, drift, drip, drop, edit, elder, element, elk, elm, emerald, end, ending, enlist, enter, ever, far, farm, fart, federal, felt, fend, fester, festival, fib, fifth, fig, finish, finger, fish, fling, flint, flip, flog, flora, flu, fluent, fluid, fog, folder, fond, for, forbid, ford, forest, forget, forever, form, format, former, fort, fossil, foster, fresh, fret, fretful, frisk, frog, from, front, frost, frugal, garden, garment, garnish, garter, get, gift, gilt, glen, go, god, goddess, godsend, gold, goldfish, golf, gorilla, government, grid, grin, grip, hard, hardship, harlot, harm, harm-

ful, harp, harsh, harvest, held, hello, help, helmet, helter-skelter, hem, hemp, hen, herald, heroin, hid, hilt, himself, hinder, hint, hip, his, hiss, historian, hit, hog, hoist, hold, honk, horn, host, hostel, hot, hotel, if, idiom, idiot, ignorant, immoral, immortal, impending, implement, import, inborn, inbred, inept, inform, inherit, ink, inlet, inn, input, insist, instant, instep, instrument, insulin, integral, intend, intent, interesting, interior, intern, Internet, interval, intolerant, invent, invest, keg, kennel, kept, kid, kilo, kilt, kin, kindergarten, king, kiosk, kip, kit, kiwi, koala, lager, lapel, lark, last, lava, led, left, leg, lemon, lend, lens, lent, lentil, leper, lesbian, lesson, lest, let, level, liberal, lid, lift, limb, limit, limp, linden, linger, lint, lip, lisp, list, lit, literal, litmus, liver, livid, living, lizard, loft, loin, loiter, long, longing, lord, lost…

I stopped with the letters starting with *l* because the list will get too long. I think you get the idea from what is listed above.

In the above, I skipped the words starting with letters *c* and *j*. I did that because in my proposed phonetic use of letters in the English alphabet I had concluded that the letter *c* should be replaced with either *k* or *s* and the letter *j* with *dsh*.

Once the letter *c* is replaced with either *k* or *s*, there will be many more words that immediately qualify as phonetically spelled words.

Words with Minor Changes

Here are samples of words where the *a* has changed to *ä* or *ö* and the *c* has changed to *k* or *s*, or some other letter has changed or has been dropped off.

In some cases, when changing the *a* to an *ä* or *ö*, the choice is somewhat difficult to make. It depends on how you are used to pronouncing the word. Some people use more of the *ä* than the *ö* sound, even though the dictionary may show the pronunciation with the *ö* sound.

Abandon – *äbändon* or *öbändon*, abhor – *äbhor* or *öbhor*, abort – *äbort* or *öbort*, absent – *äbsent*, accept – *äksept*, acid – *äsid*, admit – *ädmit*, ago – *ögo*, along – *ölong*, amend – *ämend* or *ömend*, amongst – *ömongst*, an – *än*, analog – *änälog*, ant – *änt*, anvil – *änvil*, apt – *äpt*, arc – *ark*, as – *äs*, asterisk – *ästerisk*, cadet – *kadet*, car – *kar*, cargo – *kargo*, cart – *kart*, cat – *kät*, center – *senter*, citrus – *sitrus*, civilian – *sivilian*, clever – *klever*, coma – *koma*, coroner – *koroner*, credit – *kredit*, crib – *krib*, crisp – *krisp*, critic – *kritik*, cross – *kros*, cut – *kat*, damp – *dämp*, daring – *däring*, debt – *det*, depart – *dipart*, deposit – *diposit*, detest – *ditest*, dirt – *dört*, dis-

rupt – *disrapt*, distinct – *distinkt*, do – *du*, dot – *dat*, draft – *dräft*,
dress – *dres*, drunk – *drank*, dwell – *dwel*, egg – *eg*, else – *els*, entry
– *entri*, epic – *epik*, event – *ivent*, evict – *evikt*, exit – *eksit*, extent –
ekstent, extra – *ekstra*, fabric – *fäbrik*, faint – *feint*, fat – *fät*, filthy –
filthi, fir – *för*, fitness – *fitnes*, fix – *fiks*, flag – *fläg*, flick – *flik*, frank
– *fränk*, gag – *gäg*, gap – *gäp*, garlic – *garlik*, gasp – *gäsp*, girl –
görl, give – *giv*, glut – *glat*, grain – *grein*, gulf – *galf*, hand – *händ*,
he – *hi*, hill – *hil*, horny – *horni*, housing – *hausing*, hump – *hamp*,
indirect – *indirekt*, infinity – *infiniti*, inland – *inländ*, instruct –
instrakt, intellect – *intelekt*, intestine – *intestin*, into – *intu*…

And there are many more words that require just minor changes. It
would take a dictionary to list all those words.

Words with More Difficult Changes

The Simpel-Fonetik spelling of words in the following list may not always represent precisely the tones and nuances that you are using in your pronouncing and speaking. Your pronunciations, if you are an American, will be different from the person in the United Kingdom or in India.

That is what makes the conversion of some words to phonetic spelling more difficult, requiring more thought and judgment.

In making choices between the *ä* and *ö* sounds, for example, there comes the question: Should one favor the British or the American pronunciation? The British seem to use more *ö* sounds and less *ä* sounds than the Americans and most foreigners.

The Brits also tend to leave the *r* out more than the Americans. That becomes obvious when one compares the pronunciation guidance in dictionaries that are based on British English with dictionaries that are based on American English.

In my selections between the *ä* and the *ö*, I tried not to favor any particular accent or dialect. I selected what sounded best or closest to the pronunciation that I thought was most prevalent.

But I admit that in deciding to have or not to have the letter *r* in some questionable cases, I was influenced by my empathy toward the non-native English speakers and learners. I wanted the word to sound right when a learner of English, someone who has not yet developed a dialect, pronounces the word.

My thinking was that the experienced speakers, when they read the Simpel-Fonetik words, will pronounce them the way they are used to. I thought that they will not be picky; they've had to deal with the present spelling.

It is important to keep in mind that the rule of one and only one sound for each letter applies to all conversions.

And remember the second rule: For long vowels and stronger consonants we write two of the same letter.

In the application of the second rule, one comes across cases where it is not clear if a vowel or consonant should be written with one or two letters. In questionable cases, I tilt toward the use of only one letter, as long as the word still sounds okay with the single letter—when pronounced phonetically, as a student of English would. If it does not, I will add the second letter.

Let's review some of the letters and their Simpel-Fonetik sounds.

A as in *art*   *E* as in *ten*   *G* as in *go*   *H* as in *hotel*

I as in *in*   *J* as the *y* in *yes*   *O* as in *on*   *U* as in *put*

Ä as in *ant*   *Ö* as the *i* in *sir*

When you see two or more vowels side by side, each of them needs to be pronounced individually. Avoid the temptation to pronounce them as you may have gotten used to doing.

Here are some more samples of words converted to Simpel-Fonetik spelling:

Ability – *äbiliti,* about – *öbaut,* abreast – *öbrest,* absence – *äbsens,* academy – *äkädemi,* accidental – *äksidental,* aching – *eiking,* actress – *äktres,* administrator – *ädministreitor,* adoption – *ödapshon,* advertisement – *ädvörtaisment,* afterwards – *äfterwards,* ahead – *öhed,* alphabet – *alfabet,* amusing – *ömjusing,* angry – *ängri,* applaud – *öplood,* athletic – *äthletik,* automatic – *automätik,* awning – *ooning,* axis – *äksis,* baby – *beibi,* bachelor – *bätshelor,* badge – *bädsh,* bath – *bäth,* bathe – *beith,* bean – *biin,* been – *bin,* belch – *beltsh,* biased – *baiäsd,* blind – *blaind,* bookkeeping – *bukkiiping,* boy scout – *boi skaut,* brilliant – *briljant,* burglar – *börglar,* calculator – *kälkjuleitor,* camouflage – *kämöflaash,* cartoon – *kartuun,* certain – *sörtn,* childhood – *tshaildhud,* city – *siti,* claw – *klo,* cologne – *koloun,* come – *kam,* computer – *kompjuter,* congratulations – *kongrätjuleishöns,* copycat – *kopikät,* crazy – *kreizi,* dad – *däd,* dear – *dier,* delight – *dilait,* demonstrate – *demonstreit,* destroy – *distroi,* detachment – *ditätshment,* devotion – *divoushn,* disobey – *disobei,* divide – *divaid,* divorce – *divors,* done – *dan,* dozen – *dazn,* draught beer – *dräft bier,* dwarf – *dworf,* dyslexia – *disleksia,* earn – *örn,* either – *iither,* electrical – *elektrikal,* engine – *endshin,* engineering – *endshineering,* exam – *iksäm,* exit – *eksit,* fall – *fool,* faith – *feith,* fantasy – *fäntasi,* fasten – *fäsn,* feather – *fether,* fiasco – *fiasko,* flower – *flauer,* flying – *flaing,* foreign – *forin,* garbage – *garbidsh,* generation – *dshenereishön,* goggle – *gagl,* good – *gud,* grandpa – *grändpa,* groove – *gruv,* gynecologist – *gainekolodshist,* handle – *händl,* heal – *hiil,* housewife – *hauswaif,* hybrid – *haibrid,* ice – *ais,* incidental – *insidental,* inquiry – *inkwairi,* jacket – *dshäket,* jot – *dshat,* juice – *dshus,* jury – *dshuri,* keep – *kiip,* kilowatt – *kilowat,* kneel – *niil*, large – *lardsh*, laughing – *läfing*, legal – *liigal*, life – *laif*, liquid – *likwid*, lingerie – *ländsheri*, liquor – *likör*, love – *lav*, lyric – *lirik*, make – *meik*, manufacture – *mänufäktshör*, many – *meni*, marital – *märital*, mechanical – *mikänikal*, microscope – *maikroskoup*, motorboat – *motorbout*, myopia – *maiopia*, nation – *neishon*, nationalist – *näshionalist*, neighbor – *neibor*, news – *nuus*, note – *nout*, nourishing – *nörishing*, olympic – *olimpik*, orchid – *orkid*, outweigh – *autwei*, owner – *ouner*, panic – *pänik*, paste – *peist*, peace – *piis*, perfect – *pörfekt*, pew – *pju*, phone – *foun*, policeman – *polismän*, prank – *pränk*, prejudice – *predshudis*, prophetic – *profetik*, psychiatry – *saikaietri*, quail – *kweil*, quantity – *kwantiti* or *kwontiti*, queen – *kwiin*, radiate – *reidieit*, ranch – *räntsh*, read – *riid*, ready – *redi*, receipt – *risiit*, regular – *regjular*, renew – *rinju*, research – *risörtsh*, restaurant – *restorant* or *restoran*, right – *rait*, rough – *raf*, said – *sed*, salt – *solt*, satellite – *sätelait*, saw – *soo*, seizure – *siishör*, serve – *sörv* or *sööv*, sew – *sou*, sidewalk – *saidwook*, skyscraper – *skaiskreiper*, snore – *snor*, soon – *suun*, squeeze – *skwiis*, statue – *stätshu*, straw – *stroo*, struggle – *stragl*, suit – *suut*, suite – *swiit*, synagogue – *sinagog*, take – *teik*, taught – *toot*, tea – *tii*, thanks – *thänks*, there – *thär*, through – *thru*, touch – *tatsh*, training – *treining*, troop – *trup*, turn – *törn* or *töön*, typewriter – *taipraiter*, uncle – *ankel*, up – *ap*, united – *junaited*, vandalize – *vändalais*, verse – *vörs*, view – *vju*, volume – *voljum*, waffle – *wafl*, walk – *wook*, water – *woter*, we – *wi*, whale – *weil*, what – *wat*, when – *wen*, which – *witsh*, white – *wait*, whole – *houl*, why – *wai*, workman – *wörkmän*, wrath – *räth*, wrong – *rong*, yacht – *jaht*, yard – *jard*, year – *jier*, yes – *jes*, you – *ju*, youth – *juuth*, zeal – *ziil*, zero – *ziro*, zinc – *zink*, zipper – *ziper*, zoo – *zuu*.

Phonetic Writing

Rules for Writing

Here is a basic list of rules for writing in Simpel-Fonetik English.

- *Each letter shall represent only one spoken sound.*
- *For longer vowels and stronger consonants, use double letters—just add another letter with the same sound.*
- The letters *B, D, F, K, L, M, N, P, V, and Z* are sounded as in present English and in the International Alphabet.
- The single sounds selected for the other letters of the alphabet also conform with the International Alphabet. The descriptions of the selected sounds and the rules for converting present English spelling to the Simpel-Fonetik spelling are summarized in the following.
- *A* is used for the *a* sounds that are easily seen and heard in words like *art, car,* and *alfa.* But you need to use the letter *a* also in words where the letter *a* does not show up, like *done – dan, come – kam, fun – fan, up – ap, rough – raf, fowl – faul, dry – drai,* and *money – mani.*
- *Ä* is used for the sound of *a* as in *ant – änt, fat – fät, man – män, happy – häpi, angry – ängri, bad – bäd,* and *exam – iksäm.* It is also used for words like *chair – tshär, bare – bär, square – skwär, fair – fär,* and *various – väriös.*

- *C* is not used in Simpel-Fonetik. It is replaced by *k* as in *can – kän*, by *s* as in *cent – sent*, and by *tsh* as in *chip – tship*.

- *E* is used only for the sound of *e* as in *enter, echo, men, ten,* and *get*. Do not use it for the *i* sound as it is presently done in words like *me, tree, repeat,* and *zero*. They will be written as *mi, tri, ripiit,* and *ziro*.

- *G* is used as in *go, get, gun, log,* and *big*. Do not use *g* in words like *gin, large,* or *laugh*. They will be written as *dshin, lardsh,* and *läf*. Use *dsh* also in place of *g* in words like *gender – dshender* and *binge – bindsh*.

- *H* is used as in *hotel* and *he*. Do not use it in *photo*, with *c* as in *chin*, or as a silent letter in *right*. Those will be spelled as *foto, tshin,* and *rait*.

- *I* is used for the sound of *i* as in *India, pin, rim, mint,* and *give*. Do not use it as in *mine, climb,* and *kind*. There you need to add an *a*. Those words will be written as *main, klaim,* and *kaind*. Also use *i* in place of *y* in words like *typical – tipikal, symbol – simbol,* and *lynx – links*. Use *ii* (double *i*) in words like *read – riid, ear – iir, fear – fiir, rear – riir, deep – diip, leer – liir,* and *peer – piir*.

- *J* is used for the sound that presently is conveyed by the letter *y*, as in *you* and *young*. Write those words as *ju* and *jang*. Use *dsh* in place of *j* in words like *Jim – Dshim, join – dshoin, jungle – dshangl,* and *job – dshob*.

- *K* is used as it is now, but it also replaces *c* in words like *cat – kät, cuss – kas, sect – sekt,* and *zinc – zink*.

- *O* is used for the sound that is in *on, of, go, more, golf,* and *open*. It is also used in place of *a* in words like *tall – tool* and *water – woter*, in place of *au* in words like *taut – toot* and *maudlin – moodlin*, in place of *aw* in words like *raw – roo* and *pawn – poon*. Do not use *o* for the *u* sound that is in *two – tu* and *foot – fut*, or for the *a* sound as in *done – dan* and *love – lav*.

- $Ö$ is used in place of the letter a when it appears in words like *ago – ögo, another – önather, awhile – öwail, alike – ölaik,* and for the sounds of *or, ur, ir, er,* and *ear* in words like *word – wörd, turn – törn, stir – stör, her – hör,* and *learn – lörn.*

- Q is not used in Simpel-Fonetik. It is nearly always replaced by *kw.* Use **kw** in place of *qu* in words like *quit – kwit, quite – kwait,* and *quart – kwort.* In words like *liquor* and *parquet,* the *qu* should be replaced by just *k* to become *likör* and *parkei.*

- R is often silent or hardly pronounced at all in present English. When converting to Simpel-Fonetik, the letter *r* should be left in the word when it is usually pronounced by most speakers, or to make the word better to understand, or to distinguish it from similar words, or when it is felt that it should be pronounced to conform with other languages. There should be no silent *r.* All letters, including *r,* will be pronounced in Simpel-Fonetik.

- S is used as in *sit, ask,* and *kiss.* S also replaces the *c* in words like *civil – sivil, nice – nais,* and *cent – sent.*

- T is used as it is now, except that it should be left out of words like *creation* and *mention* where the *t* sound is not heard. Those words should be spelled as *krieishön* and *menshön.*

- U is used for the sound that is in words like *put – put, you – ju, to – tu,* and *foot – fut.* Use it also in *new – nu, two – tu, food – fuud, prove – pruuv,* and in some other combinations of letters that sound like *u.* Do not use it as it is presently used in place of *a* as in *cup – kap* and *but – bat,* or to sound like *o* as in *bought – boot,* or to sound like *ä* as in *laugh – läf.*

- W is used as it is now in *win, west,* and *swim.* It must not be used when it is not pronounced, as in *write – rait, low – lou,* and straw – *stroo.*

- X is not used in Simpel-Fonetik. It is replaced by the letters *ks* in nearly all cases. Use **ks** in place of *x* in words like *six – siks, axe – äks,* and *text – tekst.*

- *Y* is not used in Simpel-Fonetik. It is replaced by *j, i,* or *ai.*
  Use *j* in place of *y* in words like *you – ju* and *young – jang.*
  Use *i* in place of *y* in words like *typical – tipikal, symbol – simbol,* and *lynx – links.*
  Use *ai* in place of *y* in words like *my – mai, stye – stai,* and *pry – prai.*
  Use *ei* in place of *ay* in words like *may – mei, tray – trei,* and *lay – lei.*
  Use *oi* in place of *oy* in words like *annoy – annoi, boy – boi,* and *royal – roial.*
- Use *ai* also in words like *time – taim, sign – sain, rice – rais,* and *item – aitem.*
- Use *ei* also in words like *make – meik, rain – rein, sane – sein,* and *frame – freim.*
- Use *au* in words like *house – haus, loud – laud, how – hau, town – taun.*
- Use *ou* in words like *foam – foum, comb – koum, most – moust, zone – zoun, low – lou,* and *sew – sou.*
- Use *sh* in place of *s* in words like *sugar – shugar* and *sure – shur,*
  in place of *ch* in words like *machine – mäshiin* and *cache – käsh,*
  in place of *ti* in words like *nation – neishon* (or *neishn*) and *devotion – divoushn,*
  in place of *ss* in words like *tissue – tishu* and *passion – päshon,*
  in place of *sc* in words like *conscience – kanshens* and *crescendo – kreshendo,*
  in place of *ce* in words like *ocean – oushan* and *facial – feishal,*
  in words like *garage – garaash, pleasure – pleshör,* and *vision – vishön,*
  and continue to use it in words like *shim – shim, cash – käsh,* and *fashion – fäshön.*
- Use *dsh* in place of *j* in words like *Jim – Dshim, join – dshoin,*

and *jungle – dshangl*. Also in place of *g* in words like *gender – dshender* and *binge – bindsh* and *manage – mänidsh*.

- Use **tsh** in place of *ch, tch,* and *tu* in words like *chin – tshin, such – satsh, pitch – pitsh, catch – kätsh, statue – stätshu,* and *nature – neitshö*.
- Use **ks** in place of *x,* in words like *six – siks* and *text – tekst,* and in place of *cc* in words like *accent – äksent* and *vaccine – väksiin*.
- Use **kw** in place of *qu* in words like *quit – kwit,* and in place of *ch* in words like *choir – kwair,* but not in words like *chorus – korus* or *chore – tshor*.

The practice of spelling a word differently or adding a silent letter to distinguish meanings when the word is written but pronouncing it the same way must never be attempted in the phonetic spelling method. That practice is incompatible with the principle of phonetic spelling. If you add or change a letter, that word will be pronounced differently. It won't be the same word.

When converting the present spelling to Simpel-Fonetik, especially when establishing preferred or standard spellings, consider these guidelines: (1) When a word has variations in pronunciation, resulting in a choice of spellings, choose the spelling that is most similar to the present spelling. (2) When a word, or a similar version, is in popular use in other languages, strive toward standardization. Try to maintain similarity. (3) Strive to remedy situations where words with different meanings and spellings are pronounced the same way. Consider a slightly different pronunciation for one of the meanings. Example: convert *there* to *thär* but leave *their* as it is now.

Enunciation Practice

In England is a town named *Leicester*. That is the way the name of the town is written, but it is pronounced *Lester*. The three letters, *eic*, are "silent"—they serve no useful, reasonable purpose, as far as I can tell.

I am citing this as another example of the fact that people who are used to writing and reading English are also used to ignoring letters in a word. They are used to the fact that most letters can be pronounced in different ways. Therefore, they are more used to looking at a word as a whole, not at individual letters in the word. That is about the only way one can handle the pronunciations of *you* and *ewe*, which are pronounced identically. Looking at the individual letters just will not work.

Therefore, one should not expect a typical English speaker to know how to enunciate, how to sound out letters in a word. It would be a new experience. It would require some learning and practice.

The use of the Simpel-Fonetik writing method requires that you know how to enunciate. You need it for two purposes: (1) to pronounce a word correctly, and (2) to spell a word.

Here is a brief lesson on enunciation. It is a bit oversimplified.

If you already know how to sound out each letter in a word phonetically, you can skip the following exercises.

Pronounce the word *on*. Notice that it is made up of two sounds,
the *o* sound and the *n* sound. Pronounce the *o* and then the *n* sound.
Pronounce them separately. Then pronounce them one after the
other with hardly any separation between the two sounds. That
should come close to enunciating *on*.

Now try the word *if*. Pronounce first the *i* sound, then the *f*
sound. Don't pronounce *i* as *ai*. Pronounce it as it actually sounds
in *if*. Then say *i* and *f* quickly one after another.

Let's try the word *bed*. Pronounce each letter separately. Don't
say *bee, ee, dee (bii, ii, dii)*. Say *bh, eh, dh*. Now say them one after
another, with small spaces between the sounds.

Do the same with the word *ending*. Again, sound out each letter
separately, one after another. As you do it more rapidly, the individual sounds should formulate the word—much more distinctly than
you are used to saying it. If that is the case, you are enunciating.

End of lesson.

People who have studied other languages, especially phonetic
languages such as Estonian and Finnish or an almost phonetic language such as German, are familiar with sounding out every letter
in the word. In a phonetic language every written word not only
conveys a meaning, but serves also as its own pronunciation guide,
or key. You just read the word as it is written. But you have to make
sure that you sound out every letter in the word, just like you presently have to do when you read the pronunciation guidance that is
written with the International Phonetic Alphabet.

Sample Sentences

You have seen how words are converted to the Simpel-Fonetik spelling. Now let's read some samples of the proposed Simpel-Fonetik writing. Here is a sample:

> *This is interesting: No federal government order or effort so far for ending the helter-skelter spelling. Don't beg or long for it. It's hard for the big gorilla tu start implementing spelling dogma. It wil linger, limp, loiter, swing from pillar tu post...*

Did you have any difficulties reading the Simpel-Fonetik writing? Of course not. Did you notice any changes? There were two: *tu* instead of *to*, and *wil* instead of *will*.

The above writing was intended to illustrate and emphasize that with the Simpel-Fonetik spelling much of the present writing will stay as it is now. The Simpel-Fonetik retains the existing good spelling. It corrects only the words that use letters in violation of the single-sound-per-letter rule.

Now let's try to read some common expressions and short sentences where the changes in spelling are more noticeable.

Gud morning!

Hau ar ju?

Fain, änd ju?

Ai niid kofi, keik [cake], änd milk.

Hau matsh das this kost?

Ten dollars.

Ai häv käsh.

Let's kaunt.

Wan, tu, thri, foor, faiv, siks, seven, eit, nain, ten.

Thänk ju!

Ju ar welkam.

Pliis, kam [come] visit as [us] ögen [again] sam [some] dei.

Gud-bai!

Unless you happen to be an Estonian or a Finn, already familiar with phonetic spelling, the above short sentence samples may look strange to you.

"No way! I'll never get used to it," you might mumble under your breath.

"And the Americans will never go for it," you might say.

But many people have made statements like that whenever something new and better was introduced. Nearly everyone now uses a computer, but I remember how many people swore that they'd never need one, would never use one.

Let's not forget: The purpose of the Simpel-Fonetik method of writing is to make it easier for everyone to write and pronounce English words. There should be no doubt or question—the spelling and pronunciation will become much simpler and easier. That fact has been proven by the experiences of Estonians, Finns, and other users of languages that are based on phonetic spelling.

All right, maybe the present spelling is already easy for you. You have gone through many spelling classes, worn out several college dictionaries, memorized all the difficult words. For you, personally, there may be little to gain. Then, please, just have an open mind on this, at least for a while. Give it a chance. For other people's sake.

Try reading the following story. Don't give up too soon. It gets easier as you go along.

Reading Practice

Äs ju riid this, rimember thät ju niid tu pei ätenshön tu iitsh leter. It mait help if ju riid ölaud, or ät liist muuv jur lips äs ju lörn tu riid this.

Anles ju ar olredi fämiliar with ö längwidsh thät häs fonetik raiting, ju wil faind this nu raiting veri streindsh. Bat thät is the keis ounli in the begining. It wount teik long tu get jusd tu it.

In the begining ai faund it streindsh tu rait this wei. It rimainded mi of the taim ai först lörnd tu rait English. Thät was veri streindsh. Ai was switshing from ö fonetik längwidsh tu ö nan-fonetik längwidsh.

Bat this switsh is not so bäd. Äs ai go ölong, raiting bikams iisier änd iisier. Ai faind thät the mor ai rait, the mor nät-shural the raiting bikams. Dshast äs in Estonian, ai ounli niid tu inansieit iitsh wörd, änd bingo, ai nou hau tu spel it.

The big sikrit tu saksess is thät iitsh saund is represented bai ö singl leter, änd iitsh leter represents ö singl saund.

Of kors, thär is ö slait prablem. Hau du ju inansieit

wörds? Wi ool tend tu inansieit wörds diferentli. Hau du ju händl diferent äksents, diferent pronansieishons in diferent kantris? Iitsh pronansieishon wil produs ö diferent spelling. Let mi tel ju hau this prablem was händld in Estonia.

In Estonia, wen the fonetik spelling was propousd, bäk öraund 1850, thär wär argjuments ögenst the propousal, bat the mädshoriti went ölong. Ö fonetik alfabet was estäblishd, ö Lätin alfabet beisd on wan leter for iitsh saund änd wan saund pör leter. Ö dikshönäri with the propousd nu spelling was isjud, änd from thär on, the raiting änd pronaunsing divelopd nätshurali.

Estonia häd meni äksents änd daiälekts bifor the nu fonetik spelling was introdusd. Änd thär ar still several daiälekts eksisting. The nu fonetik spelling did not bather the daiälekts. Thär was no intent tu du öwei with daiälekts.

Äkshuäli, the nu fonetik spelling helpd prisörv the daiälekts. The daiälekt wörds kud nau bi ritn daun änd pronaunsd olweis the seim wei, änd olso forin wörds änd nu wörds wär meid iisili riidbl änd pronaunsabl.

The raiting of sam Estonian wörds was kwestshond, änd ai äm shur thät in mai raiting the selekshon of sam leters wil bi kwestshond. For eksämpl, it mei bi argjud thät the wörd *was* shud bi speld *wos*, with än *o* insted of än *a*. Bat ai häv hörd pronansieishöns of *was* thät saunded klouser tu the fonetik *a* saund. So ai tshous not tu tsheindsh the spelling of *was*.

It wil bi kwestshond, "Arnt wi tsheindshing the English pronansieishon with this nu spelling?" Thät is ö gud kwestshon. The änser is: Meibi. It dipends on the pörson hu is riiding. If the pörson is veri prisais in inansieiting leters, his riiding of the fonetik raiting mei saund slaitli diferent from his riiding the present raiting.

This häpend in Estonia wen the nu fonetik raiting was put tu jus. The spiiking ödshasted tu the raiting. Thär was no longer än ansörtänti or lätitjud in pronaunsing wörds. Iitsh leter häd ö distinkt, wel-noun saund. If ju mispronaunsd samthing, ju häd meid a misteik in riiding the wörd. Thär wär no tu weis of pronaunsing samthing.

Ai ekspekt the seim thing tu häppen wen this propousd raiting is jusd. Thär wil bi mor prisais änd juniform pronansieishon of wörds. Änd mor prisais pronansieishon wil liid to greiter iis of spelling. It wil olso liid tu beter komjunikeishon bitwiin piipl.

Let mi dshast sei thät wen this propousd tsheindsh is ödapted änd piipl get fämiliar with it, thei wil häv hardli eni trabl in raiting English, in spelling wörds korrektli. The English dikshönäris, bi thei kalidsh or forin längwidsh dikshönäris, wil nat niid tu inkluud pronansieishon info. Skuuls wil not spend miljons of aurs on tiitshing spelling änd pronansieishon, änd raiters änd spiikers wil not niid tu riför tu ö dikshönäri for spelling or pronansieishon gaidans.

I presume that you read [red] and understood the above short story.

Based on my own experiences, I can say that if your background includes the study of Latin or Latin alphabet-based foreign languages, you managed to read [riid] it without difficulties. If you have learned how to read correctly such Latin sayings as *e pluribus unum* (one out of many) and *per aspera ad astra* (through difficulties toward the stars), you have the basic background for reading the Simpel-Fonetik writing.

People who have studied foreign languages have another advantage. They realize that the reading of any new, differently written material takes some getting used to. It took me a long time to get used to reading English. It was easier for me to read German than English. I was held back by the inconsistent and confusing spelling of English words. That problem, of course, will be eliminated by the Simpel-Fonetik writing, and English will be easier to read than German.

If you happen to be someone who has not studied foreign languages, please try the following experiment. Some time later, read the preceding Simpel-Fonetik sample story again. And read it again in a day or two. You'll notice that every time you read it again, you get more used to the writing. After a while you read it as naturally as you read this writing.

For the benefit of those few readers who may be inescapably attached to the present English spelling and who may have skipped the preceding short story in Simpel-Fonetik writing, here is the "translation" of the story in the present English spelling.

> As you read this, remember that you need to pay attention to each letter. It might help if you read aloud, or at least move your lips as you learn to read this.
>
> Unless you are already familiar with a language that has phonetic writing, you will find this new writing very strange. But that is the case only in the beginning. It won't take long to get used to it.
>
> In the beginning I found it strange to write this way. It reminded me of the time I first learned to write English. That was very strange. I was switching from a phonetic language to a non-phonetic language.

But this switch is not so bad. As I go along, writing becomes easier and easier. I find that the more I write, the more natural the writing becomes. Just as in Estonian, I only need to enunciate each word, and bingo, I know how to spell it.

The big secret to success is that each sound is represented by a single letter, and each letter represents a single sound.

Of course, there is a slight problem. How do you enunciate words? We all tend to enunciate words differently. How do you handle different accents, different pronunciations in different countries? Each pronunciation will produce a different spelling.

Let me tell you how this problem was handled in Estonia.

In Estonia, when the phonetic spelling was proposed, back around 1850, there were arguments against the proposal, but the majority went along. A phonetic alphabet was established, a Latin alphabet based on one letter for each sound and one sound per letter. A dictionary with the proposed new spelling was issued, and from there on, the writing and pronouncing developed naturally.

Estonia had many accents and dialects before the new phonetic spelling was introduced. And there are still several dialects existing. The new phonetic spelling did not bother the dialects. There was no intent to do away with dialects.

Actually, the new phonetic spelling helped preserve the dialects. The dialect words could now be written down and pronounced always the same way, and also foreign words and new words were made easily readable and pronounceable.

The writing of some Estonian words was questioned, and I am sure that in my writing the selection of some letters will be questioned. For example, it may be argued that the word *was* should be spelled *wos*, with an *o* instead of an *a*. But I have heard pronunciations of *was* that sounded closer to the phonetic *a* sound. So I chose not to change the spelling of *was*.

It will be questioned, "Aren't we changing the English pronunciation with this new spelling?" That is a good question. The answer is: Maybe. It depends on the person who is reading.

If the person is very precise in enunciating letters, his reading of the phonetic writing may sound slightly different from his reading the present writing.

This happened in Estonia when the new writing was put to use. The speaking adjusted to the writing. There was no longer an uncertainty or latitude in pronouncing words. Each letter had a distinct, well-known sound. If you mispronounced something, you had made a mistake in reading the word. There were no two ways of pronouncing something.

I expect the same thing to happen when this proposed writing is used. There will be more precise and uniform pronunciation of words. And more precise pronunciation will lead to greater ease of spelling. It will also lead to better communication between people.

Let me just say that when this proposed change is adopted and people get familiar with it, they will have hardly any trouble in writing English, in spelling words correctly. The English dictionaries, be they college or foreign language dictionaries, will not need to include pronunciation info. Schools will not spend millions of hours on teaching spelling and pronunciation, and writers and speakers will not need to refer to a dictionary for spelling or pronunciation guidance.

Implementing Reform

Why Change the Present Spelling?

The first thing that comes to my mind as the reason for changing the present spelling is that the English spelling is "broken." It is in very bad shape. It needs extensive repair or replacement. We repair or replace our cars, houses, all kinds of things—why not our language and spelling?

I have already covered the spelling problems, the "brokenness" of the spelling, in the "Problems" chapter. Books have been written on that subject. Two recently published excellent books are "Spelling Dearest," by Niall McLeod Waldman, and "Spellbound," by James Essinger. The technical details of the problems with the English spelling are well covered in those books and in other publications.

"Spelling Dearest" starts out with the statement: "According to the written testimony of a great many knowledgeable experts, the English language has by far 'the worst and most irrational and inconsistent alphabetic spelling system in the entire world'" (p. xiii).

"Spellbound" states, "Many people, whether native speakers of English or those learning English as a second language, regard English spelling as at best a joke and at worst a nightmare deliberately designed to bamboozle and perplex anyone who tries to learn it" (p. 9). It also points out that "logic in English spelling is about as rare as a joke in a dictionary" (p. 14).

The spelling system is broken. But not everyone is ready to fix something that is broken. Some people consider an old, broken down car an antique and want to keep it that way, for old time's sake. "Spellbound" concludes that there will not be any change, because the present spelling represents a cultural heritage. It ends with the statement, "We are destined to be spellbound by English spelling forever" (p. 293).

I don't accept that. I argue that if one wants to keep an antique, poorly performing car for his personal use as a remembrance of some heritage, that is fine; that's his personal matter. But here we are involved with something that does not belong to a person, nor to a nation. The English language now belongs to everyone, be they native or foreign—to everyone who is learning or using English. According to *Spellbound*, there are 350 million native English speakers, but the number of foreigners who speak English as the second language is well in excess of one billion (p. 283). There are three times more foreign than native English speakers. We are involved here with something similar to a worldwide transportation system. When that is broken, it affects everyone. Some group that likes old-fashioned, slow and rickety transportation has no right to hold back repairs and modernization and make others suffer. This analogy applies to the use of the English language. We must consider the wishes and needs of all English speakers, especially the very large number of foreign speakers and learners of English.

If the question of fixing the spelling is directed to foreigners, the ones who are learning English as a second language—people whose mother tongue is not English—then, based on my experience and background, I can say that the answer is a resounding yes. They want the spelling fixed. They don't want to put up with the difficulties and frustrations associated with the present spelling. The cultural heritage issue is not relevant to them.

I am sure that a large share, perhaps a great majority, of native English speakers would also support spelling improvements. Many people realize that their hesitancy or opposition to change is based primarily on the fact that old habits are hard to break. They have spent a lot of time learning the present spelling, and they have become used to it. Some people are excellent spellers and are proud of their spelling talent and skills. But fair-minded people realize that improvements are needed, and they realize that change is possible.

People in Great Britain had a monetary system consisting of twelve pence per shilling and twenty shillings per pound. That system had cultural heritage value, but visitors, foreigners, and financial institutions had difficulties dealing with it. The British people fixed that problem. They converted to the decimal system.

The British/American measuring system has a fascinating history. One could say that it has some cultural heritage value. The distance measuring system is based on a king's foot size. But that system is very cumbersome to use in the modern, scientifically advanced world. It is being replaced by the metric system. The field of electrical engineering, for example, has totally eliminated the inch-foot-yard-mile measuring system and uses only the metric system, or, more accurately, the mks (meter-kilogram-second) system. The progress in the electrical/electronics field could not have been possible if the theory and application of electrical engineering had been based on the historically fascinating system. The scientific and technical people understand that improvements are needed for progress. I feel that they will support a switch to a better spelling method, especially to the scientifically and logically sound Simpel-Fonetik method.

The big advantage of the Simpel-Fonetik spelling is that one can write what one hears and write it down accurately and reliably. When I say that my name is Allan and pronounce it properly, phonetically, I don't need to spell out the individual letters when I am in Estonia, Finland, Germany, or in other countries that have phonetic spelling. But when I say my name in the United States, I need to spell out the letters. That is because the name is sometimes spelled as Allen or Alan, and the non-phonetic pronunciation does not reveal the distinction—all three versions are pronounced pretty much the same way. By the way, my name came from the name of Edgar Allan Poe.

English speakers spend much time and effort in spelling their names and all kinds of words in verbal transfer of information. Much time is wasted in spelling this or that information. Many difficulties are caused by misspellings. That all is eliminated when one uses phonetic spelling.

Another big advantage of phonetic spelling is that slang and dialect expressions can be written down so that others can interpret and pronounce them correctly. One can not do it with the present English spelling because most letters have many different sounds. But it is easy to do when one uses the single-sound-per-letter writing. The writers and authors who write in phonetic languages, such as Finnish and Estonian, often include quotations in slang or dialect to make their stories more interesting and realistic. With Simpel-Fonetik writing, the English writers will also be able to do it.

New and foreign words can be written down so that one knows how to pronounce them. The pronunciation of names of products, companies, people, countries, etc. does not need to be explained. The writing serves as the pronunciation guide, or key.

The pronunciations of many English words are becoming more and more inconsistent in different English-speaking countries and especially among the new users of English. This trend is ruining the English language. The present helter-skelter spelling enables the trend. One can't expect, especially the foreign speakers of English, to have a uniform pronunciation of words when the letter *a* has eleven different sounds, the letter *o* at least seven, *e* and *u* at least six, and the *ough* combination of letters can be pronounced in at least five ways, as exemplified by the words *cough, rough, though, through,* and *plough.* The use of phonetic spelling will stop this trend. When Simpel-Fonetik spelling is used, everyone who can read will know how to pronounce words correctly, without the use of a dictionary.

The global use of the English language has expanded so much that when Americans, or other native English speakers, travel to countries that have a different language, they expect the local people to speak English to them. And the locals do that more and more, even though learning English is very difficult for them. Remember, they have to learn everything from books rather than from their parents as little children. The learning from books involves the struggle with the terrible writing of English and the confusing pronunciations of words.

Here is a good selfish reason for the native English speakers to support the change in spelling: By making English easier to learn, more foreigners will speak English. They will learn it faster and speak it better. When English speakers travel to foreign countries, they don't need to spend their time and effort to learn the local language.

I do not want to leave the impression that it is not important for the native English speakers to study foreign languages. It is very important, especially for politicians, business people, military and security officials—for anyone dealing with foreign countries—to know the language of the people they deal with. Without knowing the local language, the English speakers will not learn about and will not understand the true nature and the underlying characteristics and behavior patterns of foreigners. From that lack of understanding, people make bad decisions. Learning the local language helps to avoid that.

Learning other languages will become much easier when English speakers adopt the Simpel-Fonetik single-sound-per-letter principle. Then they can write down foreign words and their pronunciations without having to use the International Phonetic Alphabet. Learning will also become easier and faster because English writing will be based on the international (NATO) alphabet. The English letters and corresponding sounds will be the same as those used in many other languages. That is an additional important reason for changing to Simpel-Fonetik spelling.

The use of computers will become easier when writing is based on the single-sound-per-letter principle. I'll explain why, using young people as the example.

Presently, our young people are taught to associate complete words or syllables, rather than individual letters, with spoken sounds. That is because they have to deal with words like *colonel* and *kernel* and *you* and *ewe*. Looking at individual letters just does not work. However, when students learn the Simpel-Fonetik writing method, they will get used to looking at individual letters. That will make them more proficient in handling e-mail and Web page addresses and other computer entries where one must pay attention to each letter. That is a very important consideration because more and more young people are getting involved with computers and the Internet.

The American, British, and other native English speakers need to support the spelling reform out of consideration for the young minds who, in their early development years, are exposed to and are forced to deal with the English spelling. For some young minds it is very difficult to accept that in one application, spelling and pronunciation, it is all right to use letters inconsistently and illogically, but in other applications, in the use of letters with computers, mathematics, and science, letters must be used precisely and consistently. "Why? Why?" the young minds ask.

There have been indications that the incoherent, illogical spelling of English is contributing to the increased numbers of dyslexic children in the U.S. and other English-speaking countries. That alone is a good reason for repairing the "broken" spelling.

I am sure that one can come up with additional reasons, but the list here is long enough. I'll add just one additional reason: The practice of spell-checking of writings on computers will eventually become rare, if not obsolete, when phonetic spelling is used.

It is possible that some people will miss that. They might miss the joking around with spelling that is reflected in the following poem:

Spell-Checker Blues

Eye halve a spelling chequer
It came with my pea sea
It plainly marques four my revue
Miss steaks eye kin knot sea.

Eye strike a key and type a word
And weight four it two say
Weather eye am wrong oar write
It shows me strait a weigh.

As soon as a mist ache is maid
It nose bee fore two long
And eye can put the error rite
Its rarely ever wrong.

Eye have run this poem threw it
I am shore your pleased two no
Its letter perfect in it's weigh
My chequer tolled me sew.

Anonymous

Allan Kiisk

Is Gradual Change Possible?

Andrew Carnegie (1835 – 1919), the famous American industrialist and humanitarian known for his contributions to public libraries, devoted some of his time and money in trying to improve the English spelling. He gave financial support and got personally involved with the Simplified Spelling Board to carry out a gradual improvement of English spelling. Carnegie supported a gradual change because he wanted to minimize the adverse reactions.

He supported the use of *thru* for *through*, *tuf* for *tough*, and *trauf* for *trough*. Obviously, he did not care that the letter *u* would have several different sounds. He did not advocate a single-sound-per-letter phonetic spelling. Maybe that is why nearly all of his and the Simplified Spelling Board proposals died. Only the spelling *thru* has survived.

You might question if the Simpel-Fonetik spelling could be introduced gradually, incrementally, maybe changing one letter at a time, to avoid the shock of a major change.

In a language that uses the single-sound-per-letter writing, one can change a letter assigned to a specific sound by simply canceling the present letter and assigning a new letter to the sound. That change will not affect any of the other letters or sounds. It will affect only that one letter and sound. It is an important feature of phonetic spelling.

But because English does not use phonetic spelling, such a change is nearly impossible. There are only ten letters, the "good" letters listed in the chapter titled "Revising the Alphabet," that could be changed because they have single sounds and are not tied to other letters. But those letters we don't want to change. They are already well suited for phonetic spelling.

The letters that need changes are the sixteen multi-sound letters, and that includes all English vowels. The problem with those letters is that they are used in combination with other letters, two or more letters to represent a single sound, or a letter is used for two or more different sounds. Those letters have become so intertwined with each other that one cannot change one or a few letters at a time.

As an example, let's suppose we change the letter *e* to represent only one sound, the sound of *e* as in *men*, as a way of introducing the single-sound-per-letter idea. Then how do we spell the word *mean*, for example? The letter *e* no longer belongs there because it does not have the proper sound for that word. If you take the *e* out of there, you need something like *ii* to replace the whole *ea* combination. The word could be written as *miin*. But we have not yet standardized the *i* sound. Presently, the letter *i* has at least five different sounds. We need to standardize also the *i* sound before we can use it as replacement.

Let's suppose that we decide to use the letter *i* only for the sound of *i* as in *kit*. The use of *i* in *kit* would be correct, but it would be incorrect in *kite*. We'd have to correct that spelling. How do we now spell *kite*? Using other existing sounds and letters we could change *kite* to *kyte*, based on the use of *y* as in *my*. But *y* is also used for the *i* sound as in *typical* and for the *j* sound as in *you*. We just swapped one bad use of a letter for another.

And we can't use the *ai* substitution to make it *kait* because we have not yet standardized the *a* sound. It is a major undertaking to standardize the *a* sound. It involves the introduction of two new letters, *ä* and *ö*.

There are some minor exceptions to the intertwined letters problem. The following spelling improvements could be introduced fairly easily: replace *ph* with *f*, replace *x* with *ks,* and replace *qu* with *kw*. But those changes would amount to just minor improvements. They would not fix the overall spelling problem, the problem that many letters have multiple sounds.

The conclusion is that a gradual change to the single-sound-per-letter method of spelling English words is not feasible.

But the alternate, all-at-once change is not as bad as one might think. Remember, we are not changing the spelling of all words. There are many words in the English language that require no change that are presently spelled correctly, phonetically, based on single sound per letter, using the sounds that are standardized in the international alphabet. And there are many words that require only minor changes, such as replacing the *x* with *ks* and *ph* with *f*.

The Simpel-Fonetik method builds on the phonetically correct spelling that already exists in the English writing. The overall change could be viewed as expanding that spelling to the other, the inconsistently and illogically spelled words.

The most radical change is the addition of two letters, *ä* and *ö*, to take care of the problem that the letter *a* presently has eleven different sounds. There is no way to avoid adding at least two letters. It should be appreciated that only two letters are added, and four letters are no longer needed. The new Simpel-Fonetik spelling gets by with fewer letters than the present spelling.

But just because the technique, or the method, of phonetic spelling—the one-sound-per-letter spelling—cannot be introduced in a bit-by-bit, letter-by-letter fashion, it does not mean that the spelling reform cannot be carried out in a consensus building, step-by-step way. Here are some steps, actions, and results that I visualize and hope for.

Steps for Implementing Reform

First, there needs to be a concerted effort to develop a positive attitude toward spelling changes. The native English speakers need to be informed, educated, and convinced that change is inevitable and will benefit everyone. This will require dedicated people and financial resources. I believe that support will be available from individuals, foundations, and firms that favor advancements in human relations among people and nations and who view English as a global language.

Existing organizations that presently advocate improvements in spelling could take the lead in promoting the change. The Simplified Spelling Society, an organization with worldwide membership, based in the United Kingdom, could be one such organization. It could undertake the support and promotion of Simpel-Fonetik spelling.

Commissions could be established within the U.S., the U.K., and other nations, or within large organizations such as the United Nations and the European Union for the purpose of developing an implementation program. Organizations such as the North

Atlantic Treaty Organization (NATO), the American National Standards Institute (ANSI), and similar ones could start establishing policies, goals, and procedures for implementation.

The conversion of English to phonetic spelling should be established as a goal. All new words should be selected to be in agreement with the single-sound-per-letter principle. Names should be selected with the awareness that they will be pronounced phonetically, just like other English words, when phonetic spelling is used.

A simple, small dictionary needs to be available in the conversion and transition process, a dictionary that lists words in the present spelling and gives the corresponding Simpel-Fonetik spelling. Such a dictionary is needed especially for the purpose of establishing the preferred, or standard, spellings for those words that have multiple pronunciations. When converting those words to phonetic spelling, the question comes up: Which of those pronunciations should be selected for Simpel-Fonetik writing? Remember, when we use phonetic writing, each variation in pronunciation results in a different spelling. The dictionary will provide the answer; it will show the spelling that is preferred for formal and official writing. The selection of the preferred spellings must be done with great awareness of worldwide use and should be based on the guidelines given in this book in the chapter titled "Phonetic Writing" (p. 117).

The writers and publishers of English lexicons, college, and foreign language dictionaries have an important role in implementing phonetic spelling. As the very first step, they should start using the Simpel-Fonetik alphabet and spelling method for pronunciation keys and guidance. That would help the native English speakers to get used to the single-sound-per-letter spelling method. And for the non-native English speakers it will be a relief to see letters used the way they are used in many other languages and in the international (NATO) alphabet. The present usage of *a* as the key for the *at* sound, *ä* for the *a* as in *father* sound, *oo* as the key for the *u* sound in *school*, *u* as the key for the *a* sound in *up*, and *ur* for the *ö* sound in *urge* ignores the international usage of those letters and the problems caused by letters that have multiple sounds.

Sooner or later, lexicons and college dictionaries are expected to be published in Simpel-Fonetik writing and distributed for worldwide use.

In countries that already use phonetic or nearly phonetic spelling, such as Estonia, Finland, Germany, Spain, Portugal, Mexico, and others, the phonetic spelling of English will be readily accepted because people are aware of the advantages of the single-sound-per-letter writing method. The teachers in those countries know that the teaching of English will be simpler and the learning process more rapid and less frustrating. I feel that the Simpel-Fonetik spelling has the best chance of being introduced and promulgated in those countries.

It will be more difficult to introduce the phonetic spelling in the English-speaking countries, such as the United States and Great Britain. In those countries, the teaching of phonetic spelling could be introduced on a gradual basis. The teachers of languages, English and foreign languages, could introduce the Simpel-Fonetik single-sound-per-letter writing method by first using it for pronunciation guidance, to explain how English or foreign words are pronounced. Simpel-Fonetik is much easier to use and for students to learn than the International Phonetic Alphabet. As familiarity is gained with the single-sound-per-letter writing method, it could be introduced in basic English spelling and pronunciation courses as the new way of spelling English. The teaching method, of course, will have to change—students need to be taught to associate letters rather than words or syllables with spoken sounds. For teachers this will be a big change. But for students it will have a big payoff: Spelling and pronouncing will be much simpler. And the idea of concentrating on individual letters rather than words or syllables will help the students in the use of computers and in dealing with scientific terms and learning other languages.

I suspect that Internet users will quickly embrace the Simpel-Fonetik spelling. All kinds of symbols and abbreviations are being introduced to make writing easier. The people and groups who are already pursuing the simplification efforts could now start supporting the single-sound-per-letter idea. I see nothing wrong in starting to use the Simpel-Fonetik writing gradually in casual, informal correspondence and other writings. That would help to get used to the single-sound-per-letter writing method. One could start with expressions like *gud morning, gud-bai, pliis,* and *thänk ju,* and use *f* in place of *ph* in words like *foto* and *alfabet, ks* in place of *x* in words like *tekst* and *seks,* and *kw* in place of *qu* in words like *kwit* and *kwik.*

Some Internet-related company could provide the impetus for the spelling change by converting some of its writings to Simpel-Fonetik.

The new phonetically spelled English could be referred to as the international version, because it is based on the international alphabet. For some time to come, the international version could develop in coexistence with the present, the old version, which could be called the classical version. Official large-scale conversions to the international version could take place as agreed upon by individual countries or organizations, such as the United Nations and the European Union.

Let's Do It

There were terrible outcries against Andrew Carnegie's proposals to reform the English spelling. Other proposals to change the spelling have failed. Therefore, it seems reasonable to question why the spelling reform proposed in this book would not have the same fate.

The answer is that this proposal is different from the previous ones in several ways. For one thing, the proposed Simpel-Fonetik spelling change takes into account, and is more cognizant of, the international and global use of the English language. It tries to create greater harmony and blending-in with other languages. The sounds in the Simpel-Fonetik alphabet are the same as those that are used in many other languages. They conform with the sounds assigned to the letters in the standard international (NATO) alphabet.

Secondly, the spelling method, or technique, is different from those that have been proposed before. It is based on the *keep it simple* principle. Instead of increasing the number of letters in the alphabet, which has been necessary with other proposals, the Simpel-Fonetik reduces it. The single-sound-per-letter idea itself is not new—even Benjamin Franklin thought of it—but the reliance on existing letters, and the borrowing of two letters from other popular alphabets, is different. And the use of the fully phonetic Estonian and Finnish languages as examples and experimental proof of the great advantages of the Simpel-Fonetik spelling is unique.

Thirdly, in recent years, there has been a phenomenal increase in the use of the English language. For example, upon the collapse of the Soviet Union, English has become the most important foreign language in Estonia, Latvia, Lithuania, Poland, Hungary, and other countries that were previously behind the iron curtain.

The number of non-native English speakers has grown rapidly. And so has the number of people who are frustrated with and complain about the English spelling. That situation cannot, and must not, be ignored. The spelling problems need to be corrected.

I fervently hope that the primary users of the English language, Great Britain and the United States, will find the strength to undertake the task of creating common sense and logic in English spelling.

This book will help to do that. It provides the necessary groundwork and the basic rules for implementing a practical and proven solution to the spelling and pronunciation problems of the English language.

All that is needed now is the willingness and commitment to get started with the changes.

Let's start.

Let's du it nau.

Bibliography

1. Anderson, G. B. *The Forgotten Crusader: Andrew Carnegie and the simplified spelling movement.* Journal of the Simplified Spelling Society, J26, 1999/2, pp. 11–15.
2. Ehala, Martin. *Eesti Kirjakeel. Gümnaasiumi Õigekeelsusõpik. (Estonian Writing. High School Textbook).* Künnimees, Estonia, 1998.
3. Essinger, James. *Spellbound:The Surprising Origins and Astonishing Secrets of English Spelling.* Bantam Dell: New York, N.Y., 2007.
4. Hint, Mati. *Eesti keele foneetika ja morfoloogia. (Estonian language phonetics and morphology).* Avita, Estonia, 2004.
5. Waldman, Niall McLeod. *Spelling Dearest: The Down and Dirty Nitty-Gritty History of English Spelling.* What The Dickens Press: Bloomington, IN, 2004.